Warfighting

U.S. Marine Corps

PCN 142 000006 00

DEPARTMENT OF THE NAVY
Headquarters United States Marine Corps
Washington, D.C. 20380-1775

20 June 1997

FOREWORD

Since Fleet Marine Force Manual 1, *Warfighting*, was first
published in 1989, it has had a significant impact both inside
and outside the Marine Corps. That manual has changed the
way Marines think about warfare. It has caused energetic
debate and has been translated into several foreign languages,
issued by foreign militaries, and published commercially. It has
strongly influenced the development of doctrine by our sister
Services. Our current naval doctrine is based on the tenets of
maneuver warfare as described in that publication. Current
and emerging concepts such as operational maneuver from the
sea derive their doctrinal foundation from the philosophy
contained in *Warfighting*. Our philosophy of warfighting, as
described in the manual, is in consonance with joint doctrine,
contributing to our ability to operate harmoniously with the
other Services.

That said, I believe *Warfighting* can and should be improved.
Military doctrine cannot be allowed to stagnate, especially an
adaptive doctrine like maneuver warfare. Doctrine must
continue to evolve based on growing experience, advancements

theory, and the changing face of war itself. It is in this spirit that *Warfighting* has been revised, and this publication, Marine Corps Doctrinal Publication 1, supersedes Fleet Marine Force Manual 1. I have several goals for this revision. One goal is to enhance the description of the nature of war—for example, to emphasize war's complexity and unpredictability and to widen the definition of war to account for modern conflict's expanding forms. Another goal is to clarify the descriptions of styles of warfare. A third goal is to clarify and refine important maneuver warfare concepts such as commander's intent, main effort, and critical vulnerability. It is my intent to do this while retaining the spirit, style, and essential message of the original.

Very simply, this publication describes the philosophy which distinguishes the U.S. Marine Corps. The thoughts contained here are not merely guidance for action in combat but a way of thinking. This publication provides the authoritative basis for how we fight and how we prepare to fight. This book contains no specific techniques or procedures for conduct. Rather, it provides broad guidance in the form of concepts and values. It requires judgment in application.

Warfighting is not meant as a reference manual; it is designed to be read from cover to cover. Its four chapters have a natural progression. Chapter 1 describes our understanding of the characteristics, problems, and demands of war. Chapter 2 derives a theory about war from that understanding. This theory in turn provides the foundation for how we prepare for war and how we wage war, chapters 3 and 4, respectively.

Experience has shown that the warfighting philosophy described on these pages applies far beyond the officer corps. I expect all Marines—enlisted and commissioned—to read this book, understand it, and act upon it. As General A. M. Gray stated in his foreword to the original in 1989, this publication describes a philosophy for action that, in war, in crisis, and in peace, dictates our approach to duty.

C. C. KRULAK
General, U.S. Marine Corps
Commandant of the Marine Corps

www.bnpublishing.net

info@bnpublishing.net

Throughout this publication, masculine nouns and pronouns are used for the sake of simplicity. Except where otherwise noted, these nouns and pronouns apply to either gender.

PREFACE

Eight years ago the Marine Corps published the first edition of *Warfighting*. Our intent was to describe my philosophy on warfighting, establish it as Marine Corps doctrine, and present it in an easy-to-read format. In the foreword to that manual, I charged every officer to read and reread the text, to understand it, and to take its message to heart. We have succeeded. *Warfighting* has stimulated discussion and debate from classrooms to wardrooms, training areas to combat zones. The philosophy contained in this publication has influenced our approach to every task we have undertaken.

Fleet Marine Force Manual 1 stated, "War is both timeless and ever changing. While the basic nature of war is constant, the means and methods we use evolve continuously." Like war itself, our approach to warfighting must evolve. If we cease to refine, expand, and improve our profession, we risk becoming outdated, stagnant, and defeated. Marine Corps Doctrinal

Publication 1 refines and expands our philosophy on warfighting, taking into account new thinking about the nature of war and the understanding gained through participation in extensive operations over the past decade. Read it, study it, take it to heart.

Semper Fidelis,

A. M. GRAY
General, U.S. Marine Corps (Ret.)
29th Commandant of the Marine Corps

Warfighting

Chapter 1.The Nature of War
War Defined—Friction—Uncertainty—Fluidity—
Disorder—Complexity—The Human Dimension—
Violence and Danger—Physical, Moral, and Mental
Forces—The Evolution of War—The Science, Art, and
Dynamic of War—Conclusion

Chapter 2.The Theory of War
War As an Act of Policy—Means in War—The
Spectrum of Conflict—Levels of War—Initiative
and Response—Styles of Warfare—Combat Power—
Speed and Focus—Surprise and Boldness—Centers of
Gravity and Critical Vulnerabilities—Creating and
Exploiting Opportunity—Conclusion

Chapter 3.Preparing for War
Force Planning—Organization—Doctrine—
Professionalism—Training—Professional Military
Education—Personnel Management—Equipping—
Conclusion

Chapter 4.The Conduct of War
The Challenge—Maneuver Warfare—Orienting on the
Enemy—Philosophy of Command—Shaping the Action—
Decisionmaking—Mission Tactics—Commander's Intent—
Main Effort—Surfaces and Gaps—Combined Arms—
Conclusion

Chapter 1

The Nature of War

"Everything in war is simple, but the simplest thing is difficult. The difficulties accumulate and end by producing a kind of friction that is inconceivable unless one has experienced war." [1]

—Carl von Clausewitz

"In war the chief incalculable is the human will." [2]

—B. H. Liddell Hart

"Positions are seldom lost because they have been destroyed, but almost invariably because the leader has decided in his own mind that the position cannot be held." [3]

—A. A. Vandegrift

To understand the Marine Corps' philosophy of warfighting, we first need an appreciation for the nature of war itself—its moral, mental, and physical characteristics and demands. A common view of war among Marines is a necessary base for the development of a cohesive doctrine because our approach to the conduct of war derives from our understanding of the nature of war.

WAR DEFINED

War is a violent clash of interests between or among organized groups characterized by the use of military force. These groups have traditionally been established nation-states, but they may also include any nonstate group—such as an international coalition or a faction within or outside of an existing state—with its own political interests and the ability to generate organized violence on a scale sufficient to have significant political consequences.

The essence of war is a violent struggle between two hostile, independent, and irreconcilable wills, each trying to impose itself on the other. War is fundamentally an interactive social process. Clausewitz called it a *Zweikampf* (literally a "two-struggle") and suggested the image of a pair of wrestlers locked in a hold, each exerting force and counterforce to try to throw the other.[4] War is thus a process of continuous mutual adaptation, of give and take, move and countermove. It is critical to keep in mind that the enemy is not an inanimate object to be acted upon but an independent and animate force with its own objectives and plans. While we try to impose our will on the enemy, he resists us and seeks to impose his own will on us. Appreciating this dynamic interplay between opposing human wills is essential to understanding the fundamental nature of war.

The object in war is to impose our will on our enemy. The means to this end is the organized application or threat of violence by military force. The target of that violence may be limited to hostile combatant forces, or it may extend to the enemy population at large. War may range from intense clashes between large military forces—sometimes backed by an official declaration of war—to subtler, unconventional hostilities that barely reach the threshold of violence.

Total war and perfect peace rarely exist in practice. Instead, they are extremes between which exist the relations among most political groups. This range includes routine economic competition, more or less permanent political or ideological tension, and occasional crises among groups. The decision to resort to the use of military force of some kind may arise at any point within these extremes, even during periods of relative peace. On one end of the spectrum, military force may be used simply to maintain or restore order in civil disturbances or disaster relief operations. At the other extreme, force may be used to completely overturn the existing order within a society or between two or more societies. Some cultures consider it a moral imperative to go to war only as a last resort when all peaceful means to settle disagreements have failed. Others have no such hesitancy to resort to military force to achieve their aims.

FRICTION

Portrayed as a clash between two opposing wills, war appears a simple enterprise. In practice, the conduct of war becomes extremely difficult because of the countless factors that impinge on it. These factors collectively have been called *friction*, which Clausewitz described as "the force that makes the apparently easy so difficult."[5] Friction is the force that resists all action and saps energy. It makes the simple difficult and the difficult seemingly impossible.

The very essence of war as a clash between opposed wills creates friction. In this dynamic environment of interacting forces, friction abounds.

Friction may be mental, as in indecision over a course of action. It may be physical, as in effective enemy fire or a terrain obstacle that must be overcome. Friction may be external, imposed by enemy action, the terrain, weather, or mere chance.

Friction may be self-induced, caused by such factors as lack of a clearly defined goal, lack of coordination, unclear or complicated plans, complex task organizations or command relationships, or complicated technologies. Whatever form it takes, because war is a human enterprise, friction will always have a psychological as well as a physical impact.

While we should attempt to minimize self-induced friction, the greater requirement is *to fight effectively* despite the existence of friction. One essential means to overcome friction is the will; we prevail over friction through persistent strength of mind and spirit. While striving ourselves to overcome the effects of friction, we must attempt at the same time to raise our enemy's friction to a level that weakens his ability to fight.

We can readily identify countless examples of friction, but until we have experienced it ourselves, we cannot hope to appreciate it fully. Only through experience can we come to appreciate the force of will necessary to overcome friction and to develop a realistic appreciation for what is possible in war and what is not. While training should attempt to approximate the conditions of war, we must realize it can never fully duplicate the level of friction of real combat.

UNCERTAINTY

Another attribute of war is uncertainty. We might argue that uncertainty is just one of many sources of friction, but because it is such a pervasive trait of war, we will treat it singly. All actions in war take place in an atmosphere of uncertainty, or the "fog of war." Uncertainty pervades battle in the form of unknowns about the enemy, about the environment, and even about the friendly situation. While we try to reduce these unknowns by gathering information, we must realize that we cannot eliminate them—or even come close. The very nature of war makes certainty impossible; all actions in war will be based on incomplete, inaccurate, or even contradictory information.

War is intrinsically unpredictable. At best, we can hope to determine possibilities and probabilities. This implies a certain standard of military judgment: What is possible and what is not? What is probable and what is not? By judging probability, we make an estimate of our enemy's designs and act accordingly. Having said this, we realize that it is precisely those actions that seem improbable that often have the greatest impact on the outcome of war.

Because we can never eliminate uncertainty, we must learn to fight effectively despite it. We can do this by developing simple, flexible plans; planning for likely contingencies; developing standing operating procedures; and fostering initiative among subordinates.

One important source of uncertainty is a property known as *nonlinearity*. Here the term does not refer to formations on the battlefield but describes systems in which causes and effects are disproportionate. Minor incidents or actions can have decisive effects. Outcomes of battles can hinge on the actions of a few individuals, and as Clausewitz observed, "issues can be decided by chances and incidents so minute as to figure in histories simply as anecdotes."[6]

By its nature, uncertainty invariably involves the estimation and acceptance of risk. Risk is inherent in war and is involved in every mission. Risk is equally common to action and inaction. Risk may be related to gain; greater potential gain often requires greater risk. The practice of concentrating combat power toward the main effort necessitates the willingness to accept prudent risk elsewhere. However, we should clearly understand that the acceptance of risk does not equate to the imprudent willingness to gamble the entire likelihood of success on a single improbable event.

Part of uncertainty is the ungovernable element of chance. Chance is a universal characteristic of war and a continuous source of friction. Chance consists of turns of events that cannot reasonably be foreseen and over which we and our enemy have no control. The constant potential for chance to influence outcomes in war, combined with the inability to prevent chance from impacting on plans and actions, creates psychological friction. However, we should remember that chance favors neither belligerent exclusively. Consequently, we must view chance not only as a threat but also as an opportunity which we must be ever ready to exploit.

FLUIDITY

Like friction and uncertainty, fluidity is an inherent attribute of war. Each episode in war is the temporary result of a unique combination of circumstances, presenting a unique set of problems and requiring an original solution. Nevertheless, no episode can be viewed in isolation. Rather, each episode merges with those that precede and follow it—shaped by the former and shaping the conditions of the latter—creating a continuous, fluctuating flow of activity replete with fleeting opportunities and unforeseen events. Since war is a fluid phenomenon, its conduct requires flexibility of thought. Success depends in large part on the ability to adapt—to proactively shape changing events to our advantage as well as to react quickly to constantly changing conditions.

It is physically impossible to sustain a high tempo of activity indefinitely, although clearly there will be times when it is advantageous to push men and equipment to the limit. The tempo of war will fluctuate from periods of intense combat to periods in which activity is limited to information gathering, replenishment, or redeployment. Darkness and weather can influence the tempo of war but need not halt it. A competitive rhythm will develop between the opposing wills with each belligerent trying to influence and exploit tempo and the continuous flow of events to suit his purposes.

Military forces will mass to concentrate combat power against the enemy. However, this massing will also make them vulnerable to the effects of enemy fires, and they will find it necessary to disperse. Another competitive rhythm will develop—disperse, concentrate, disperse again—as each belligerent tries to concentrate combat power temporarily while limiting the vulnerability to enemy combat power.

DISORDER

In an environment of friction, uncertainty, and fluidity, war gravitates naturally toward disorder. Like the other attributes of war, disorder is an inherent characteristic of war; we can never eliminate it. In the heat of battle, plans will go awry, instructions and information will be unclear and misinterpreted, communications will fail, and mistakes and unforeseen events will be commonplace. It is precisely this natural disorder which creates the conditions ripe for exploitation by an opportunistic will.

Each encounter in war will usually tend to grow increasingly disordered over time. As the situation changes continuously, we are forced to improvise again and again until finally our actions have little, if any, resemblance to the original scheme.

By historical standards, the modern battlefield is particularly disorderly. While past battlefields could be described by linear formations and uninterrupted linear fronts, we cannot think of today's battlefield in linear terms. The range and lethality of modern weapons have increased dispersion between units. In spite of communications technology, this dispersion strains the limits of positive control. The natural result of dispersion is unoccupied areas, gaps, and exposed flanks which can and will be exploited, blurring the distinction between front and rear and friendly- and enemy-controlled areas.

The occurrences of war will not unfold like clockwork. We cannot hope to impose precise, positive control over events. The best we can hope for is to impose a general framework of order on the disorder, to influence the general flow of action rather than to try to control each event.

If we are to win, we must be able to operate in a disorderly environment. In fact, we must not only be able to fight effectively in the face of disorder, we should seek to generate disorder and use it as a weapon against our opponent.

COMPLEXITY

War is a complex phenomenon. We have described war as essentially a clash between opposed wills. In reality, each belligerent is not a single, homogeneous will guided by a single intelligence. Instead, each belligerent is a complex system consisting of numerous individual parts. A division comprises regiments, a regiment comprises battalions, and so on all the way down to fire teams which are composed of individual Marines. Each element is part of a larger whole and must cooperate with other elements for the accomplishment of the common goal. At the same time, each has its own mission and must adapt to its own situation. Each must deal with friction, uncertainty, and disorder at its own level, and each may create friction, uncertainty, and disorder for others, friendly as well as enemy.

As a result, war is not governed by the actions or decisions of a single individual in any one place but emerges from the collective behavior of all the individual parts in the system interacting locally in response to local conditions and incomplete information. A military action is not the monolithic execution of a single decision by a single entity but necessarily involves near-countless independent but interrelated decisions and actions being taken simultaneously throughout the organization. Efforts to fully centralize military operations and to exert complete control by a single decisionmaker are inconsistent with the intrinsically complex and distributed nature of war.

THE HUMAN DIMENSION

Because war is a clash between opposing human wills, the human dimension is central in war. It is the human dimension which infuses war with its intangible moral factors. War is shaped by human nature and is subject to the complexities, inconsistencies, and peculiarities which characterize human behavior. Since war is an act of violence based on irreconcilable disagreement, it will invariably inflame and be shaped by human emotions.

War is an extreme trial of moral and physical strength and stamina. Any view of the nature of war would hardly be accurate or complete without consideration of the effects of danger, fear, exhaustion, and privation on those who must do the fighting.[7] However, these effects vary greatly from case to case. Individuals and peoples react differently to the stress of war; an act that may break the will of one enemy may only serve to stiffen the resolve of another. Human will, instilled through leadership, is the driving force of all action in war.

No degree of technological development or scientific calculation will diminish the human dimension in war. Any doctrine which attempts to reduce warfare to ratios of forces, weapons, and equipment neglects the impact of the human will on the conduct of war and is therefore inherently flawed.

VIOLENCE AND DANGER

War is among the greatest horrors known to humanity; it should never be romanticized. The means of war is force, applied in the form of organized violence. It is through the use of violence, or the credible threat of violence, that we compel our enemy to do our will. Violence is an essential element of war, and its immediate result is bloodshed, destruction, and suffering. While the magnitude of violence may vary with the object and means of war, the violent essence of war will never change.[8] Any study of war that neglects this basic truth is misleading and incomplete.

Since war is a violent enterprise, danger is ever present. Since war is a human phenomenon, fear, the human reaction to danger, has a significant impact on the conduct of war.

Everybody feels fear. Fear contributes to the corrosion of will. Leaders must foster the courage to overcome fear, both individually and within the unit. Courage is not the absence of fear; rather, it is the strength to overcome fear.[9]

Leaders must study fear, understand it, and be prepared to cope with it. Courage and fear are often situational rather than uniform, meaning that people experience them differently at different times and in different situations. Like fear, courage takes many forms, from a stoic courage born of reasoned calculation to a fierce courage born of heightened emotion. Experience under fire generally increases confidence, as can realistic training by lessening the mystique of combat. Strong leadership which earns the respect and trust of subordinates can limit the effects of fear. Leaders should develop unit cohesion and esprit and the self-confidence of individuals within the unit. In this environment, a Marine's unwillingness to violate the respect and trust of peers can overcome personal fear.

PHYSICAL, MORAL, AND MENTAL FORCES

War is characterized by the interaction of physical, moral, and mental forces. The physical characteristics of war are generally easily seen, understood, and measured: equipment capabilities, supplies, physical objectives seized, force ratios, losses of matériel or life, terrain lost or gained, prisoners or matériel captured. The moral characteristics are less tangible. (The term "moral" as used here is not restricted to ethics, although ethics are certainly included, but pertains to those forces of a psychological rather than tangible nature.)[10] Moral forces are difficult to grasp and impossible to quantify. We cannot easily gauge forces like national and military resolve, national or individual conscience, emotion, fear, courage, morale, leadership, or esprit. War also involves a significant mental, or intellectual, component. Mental forces provide the ability to grasp complex battlefield situations; to make effective estimates, calculations, and decisions; to devise tactics and strategies; and to develop plans.

Although material factors are more easily quantified, the moral and mental forces exert a greater influence on the nature and outcome of war.[11] This is not to lessen the importance of physical forces, for the physical forces in war can have a significant impact on the others. For example, the greatest effect of fires is generally not the amount of physical destruction they cause, but the effect of that physical destruction on the enemy's moral strength.

Because it is difficult to come to grips with moral and mental forces, it is tempting to exclude them from our study of war. However, any doctrine or theory of war that neglects these factors ignores the greater part of the nature of war.

THE EVOLUTION OF WAR

War is both timeless and ever changing. While the basic nature of war is constant, the means and methods we use evolve continuously. Changes may be gradual in some cases and drastic in others. Drastic changes in war are the result of developments that dramatically upset the equilibrium of war such as the rifled bore, mass conscription, and the railroad.

One major catalyst of change is the advancement of technology. As the hardware of war improves through technolo- gical development, so must the tactical, operational, and strategic usage adapt to its improved capabilities both to maximize our own capabilities and to counteract our ene- my's.

It is important to understand which aspects of war are likely to change and which are not. We must stay abreast of the process of change for the belligerent who first exploits a development in the art and science of war gains a significant advantage. If we are ignorant of the changing face of war, we will find ourselves unequal to its challenges.

THE SCIENCE, ART, AND DYNAMIC OF WAR

Various aspects of war fall principally in the realm of science, which is the methodical application of the empirical laws of nature. The science of war includes those activities directly subject to the laws of ballistics, mechanics, and like disciplines; for example, the application of fires, the effects of weapons, and the rates and methods of movement and resupply. However, science does not describe the whole phenomenon.

An even greater part of the conduct of war falls under the realm of art, which is the employment of creative or intuitive skills. Art includes the creative, situational application of scientific knowledge through judgment and experience, and so the art of war subsumes the science of war. The art of war requires the intuitive ability to grasp the essence of a unique military situation and the creative ability to devise a practical solution. It involves conceiving strategies and tactics and developing plans of action to suit a given situation. This still does not describe the whole phenomenon. Owing to the va- garies of human behavior and the countless other intangible factors which influence war, there is far more to its conduct than can be explained by art and science. Art and science stop short of explaining the fundamental dynamic of war.

As we have said, war is a social phenomenon. Its essential dynamic is the dynamic of competitive human interaction rather than the dynamic of art or science. Human beings interact with each other in ways that are fundamentally different from the way a scientist works with chemicals or formulas or the way an artist works with paints or musical notes. It is because of this dynamic of human interaction that fortitude, perseverance, boldness, esprit, and other traits not explainable by art or science are so essential in war. *We thus conclude that the conduct of war is fundamentally a dynamic process of human competition requiring both the knowledge of science and the creativity of art but driven ultimately by the power of human will.*

CONCLUSION

At first glance, war seems a simple clash of interests. On closer examination, it reveals its complexity and takes shape as one of the most demanding and trying of human endeavors. War is an extreme test of will. Friction, uncertainty, fluidity, disorder, and danger are its essential features. War displays broad patterns that can be represented as probabilities, yet it remains fundamentally unpredictable. Each episode is the unique product of myriad moral, mental, and physical forces.

Individual causes and their effects can rarely be isolated. Minor actions and random incidents can have disproportionately large—even decisive—effects. While dependent on the laws of science and the intuition and creativity of art, war takes its fundamental character from the dynamic of human interaction.

Chapter 2

The Theory of War

"The political object is the goal, war is the means of reaching it, and the means can never be considered in isolation from their purposes."[1]

—Carl von Clausewitz

"Invincibility lies in the defense; the possibility of victory in the attack. One defends when his strength is inadequate; he attacks when it is abundant."[2]

—Sun Tzu

"Battles are won by slaughter and manoeuver. The greater the general, the more he contributes in manoeuver, the less he demands in slaughter."[3]

—Winston Churchill

H aving arrived at a common view of the nature of war, we proceed to develop from it a theory of war. Our theory of war will in turn be the foundation for the way we prepare for and wage war.

WAR AS AN ACT OF POLICY

War is an extension of both policy and politics with the addition of military force.[4] Policy and politics are related but not synonymous, and it is important to understand war in both contexts. Politics refers to the distribution of power through dynamic interaction, both cooperative and competitive, while policy refers to the conscious objectives established within the political process. The policy aims that are the motive for any group in war should also be the foremost determinants of its conduct. The single most important thought to understand about our theory is that war *must serve policy*.

As the policy aims of war may vary from resistance against aggression to the unconditional surrender of an enemy government, so should the application of violence vary in accordance with those aims. Of course, we may also have to adjust our policy objectives to accommodate our chosen means. This means that we must not establish goals outside our capabilities. It is important to recognize that many political problems cannot be solved by military means. Some can, but rarely as anticipated. War tends to take its own course as it unfolds. We should recognize that war is not an inanimate instrument, but an animate force which may likely have unintended consequences that may change the political situation.

To say that war is an extension of politics and policy is not to say that war is strictly a political phenomenon: It also contains social, cultural, psychological, and other elements. These can also exert a strong influence on the conduct of war as well as on war's usefulness for solving political problems.

When the policy motive of war is extreme, such as the destruction of an enemy government, then war's natural military tendency toward destruction will coincide with the political aim, and there will tend to be few political restrictions on the military conduct of war. On the other hand, the more limited the policy motive, the more the military tendency toward destruction may be at variance with that motive, and the more likely political considerations will restrict the application of military force.[5] Commanders must recognize that since military action must serve policy, these political restrictions on military action may be perfectly correct. At the same time, military leaders have a responsibility to advise the political leadership when the limitations imposed on military action jeopardize the military's ability to accomplish its assigned mission.

There are two ways to use military force to impose our will on an enemy. The first is to make the enemy helpless to resist us by physically destroying his military capabilities. The aim is the elimination, permanent or temporary, of the enemy's military power. This has historically been called a *strategy of annihilation*, although it does not necessarily require the physical annihilation of all military forces. Instead, it requires the enemy's incapacitation as a viable military threat, and thus can also be called a *strategy of incapacitation*.[6] We use force in this way when we seek an unlimited political objective, such as the overthrow of the enemy leadership. We may also use this strategy in pursuit of more limited political objectives if we believe the enemy will continue to resist as long as any means to do so remain.

The second approach is to convince the enemy that accepting our terms will be less painful than continuing to resist. This is a *strategy of erosion*, using military force to erode the enemy leadership's will.[7] In such a strategy, we use military force to raise the costs of resistance higher than the enemy is willing to pay. We use force in this manner in pursuit of limited political goals that we believe the enemy leadership will ultimately be willing to accept.

MEANS IN WAR

At the highest level, war involves the use of all the elements of power that one political group can bring to bear against another. These include, for example, economic, diplomatic, military, and psychological forces. Our primary concern is with the use of *military force*. Nevertheless, while we focus on the use of military force, we must not consider it in isolation from the other elements of national power. The use of military force may take any number of forms from the mere deployment of forces as a demonstration of resolve to the enforcement of a negotiated truce to general warfare with sophisticated weaponry.

THE SPECTRUM OF CONFLICT

Conflict can take a wide range of forms constituting a spectrum which reflects the magnitude of violence involved. At one end of the spectrum are those actions referred to as military operations other than war in which the application of military power is usually restrained and selective. Military operations other than war encompass the use of a broad range of military capabilities to deter war, resolve conflict, promote peace, and support civil authorities. At the other end of the spectrum is general war, a large-scale, sustained combat operation such as global conflict between major powers. Where on the spectrum to place a particular conflict depends on several factors. Among them are policy objectives, available military means, national will, and density of fighting forces or combat power on the battlefield. In general, the greater this density, the more intense the conflict. Each conflict is not uniformly intense. As a result, we may witness relatively intense actions within a military operation other than war or relatively quiet sectors or phases in a major regional conflict or general war.

Military operations other than war and small wars are more probable than a major regional conflict or general war. Many political groups simply do not possess the military means to wage war at the high end of the spectrum. Many who fight a technologically or numerically superior enemy may choose to fight in a way that does not justify the enemy's full use of that superiority. Unless actual survival is at stake, political groups are generally unwilling to accept the risks associated with general war. However, a conflict's intensity may change over time. Belligerents may escalate the level of violence if the original means do not achieve the desired results. Similarly, wars may actually de-escalate over time; for example, after an initial pulse of intense violence, the belligerents may continue to fight on a lesser level, unable to sustain the initial level of intensity.

The Marine Corps, as the nation's force-in-readiness, must have the versatility and flexibility to deal with a situation at any intensity across the entire spectrum of conflict. This is a greater challenge than it may appear: Military operations other than war and small wars are not simply lesser forms of general war. A modern military force capable of waging a war against a large conventional force may find itself ill-prepared for a "small" war against a lightly equipped guerrilla force.

LEVELS OF WAR

Activities in war take place at several interrelated levels which form a hierarchy. These levels are the strategic, operational, and tactical. (See figure 1.)

The highest level is the *strategic* level.[8] Activities at the strategic level focus directly on policy objectives. Strategy applies to peace as well as war. We distinguish between *national strategy*, which coordinates and focuses all the elements of national power to attain the policy objectives,[9] and *military strategy*, which is the application of military force to secure the policy objectives.[10] Military strategy thus is subordinate to national strategy. Military strategy can be thought of as the art of winning wars and securing peace. Strategy involves establishing goals, assigning forces, providing assets, and imposing conditions on the use of force in theaters of war. Strategy derived from political and policy objectives must be clearly understood to be the sole authoritative basis for all operations.

The lowest level is the *tactical* level.[11] Tactics refers to the concepts and methods used to accomplish a particular mission

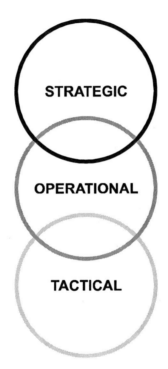

Figure 1. The Levels of War.

in either combat or other military operations. In war, tactics focuses on the application of combat power to defeat an enemy force in combat at a particular time and place. In noncombat situations, tactics may include the schemes and methods by which we perform other missions, such as enforcing order and maintaining security during peacekeeping op- erations. We normally think of tactics in terms of combat, and

29

in this context tactics can be thought of as the art and science of winning engagements and battles. It includes the use of fire-power and maneuver, the integration of different arms, and the immediate exploitation of success to defeat the enemy. Included within the tactical level of war is the performance of combat service support functions such as resupply or maintenance. The tactical level also includes the *technical* application of combat power, which consists of those techniques and procedures for accomplishing specific tasks *within* a tactical action. These include the call for fire, techniques of fire, the operation of weapons and equipment, and tactical movement techniques. There is a certain overlap between tactics and techniques. We make the point only to draw the distinction between tactics, which requires judgment and creativity, and techniques and procedures, which generally involves repetitive routine.

The *operational* level of war links the strategic and tactical levels. It is the use of tactical results to attain strategic objectives.[12] The operational level includes deciding when, where, and under what conditions to engage the enemy in battle—and when, where, and under what conditions to *refuse* battle in support of higher aims. Actions at this level imply a broader dimension of time and space than actions at the tactical level. As strategy deals with winning wars and tactics with winning battles and engagements, the operational level of war is the art and science of winning campaigns. Its means are tactical results, and its ends are the established strategic objectives.

The distinctions between levels of war are rarely clearly delineated in practice. They are to some extent only a matter of scope and scale. Usually there is some amount of overlap as a single commander may have responsibilities at more than one level. As shown in figure 1, the overlap may be slight. This will likely be the case in large-scale, conventional conflicts involving large military formations and multiple theaters. In such cases, there are fairly distinct strategic, operational, and tactical domains, and most commanders will find their activities focused at one level or another. However, in other cases, the levels of war may compress so that there is significant overlap, as shown in figure 2. Especially in either a nuclear war or a military operation other than war, a single commander may operate at two or even three levels simultaneously. In a nuclear war, strategic decisions about the direction of the war and tactical decisions about the employment

Figure 2. The Levels of War Compressed.

of weapons are essentially one and the same. In a military operation other than war, even a small-unit leader, for example, may find that "tactical" actions have direct strategic implications.

INITIATIVE AND RESPONSE

All actions in war, regardless of the level, are based upon either taking the *initiative* or reacting in *response* to the opponent. By taking the initiative, we dictate the terms of the conflict and force the enemy to meet us on our terms. The initiative allows us to pursue some positive aim even if only to preempt an enemy initiative. It is through the initiative that we seek to impose our will on the enemy. The initiative is clearly the preferred form of action because only through the initiative can we ultimately impose our will on the enemy. At least one party to a conflict must take the initiative for without the desire to impose upon the other, there would be no conflict. The second party to a conflict must respond for without the desire to resist, there again would be no conflict. If we cannot take the initiative and the enemy does, we are compelled to respond in order to counteract the enemy's attempts. The response generally has a negative aim, that of negating—blocking or counterattacking—the enemy's inten- tions. Like a counter-punch in boxing, the response often has as its object seizing the initiative from the opponent.

The flux of war is a product of the continuous interaction between initiative and response. We can imagine a conflict in which both belligerents try to take the initiative simultaneously—as in a meeting engagement, for example. After the initial clash, one of them will gain the upper hand, and the other will be compelled to respond—at least until able to wrestle the initiative away from the other. Actions in war more or less reflect the constant imperative to seize and maintain the initiative.

This discussion leads to a related pair of concepts: the *offense* and *defense*. The offense contributes *striking power*. We normally associate the offense with initiative: The most obvious way to seize and maintain the initiative is to strike first and keep striking. The defense, on the other hand, contributes *resisting power*, the ability to preserve and protect ourselves. The defense generally has a negative aim, that of resisting the enemy's will.

The defense tends to be the more efficient form of warfare—meaning that it tends to expend less energy—which is not the same as saying the defense is inherently the stronger form of warfare. The relative advantages and disadvantages of offense and defense are situationally dependent. Because we typically think of the defense as waiting for the enemy to strike, we often associate the defense with response rather than initiative. This is not necessarily true. We do not necessarily assume the defensive only out of weakness. For example, the defense may confer the initiative if the enemy is compelled to attack into the strength of our defense. Under such conditions, we may have the positive aim of destroying the enemy. Similarly, a defender waiting in ambush may have the initiative if the enemy can be brought into the trap. The defense may be another way of striking at the enemy.

While opposing forms, the offense and defense are not mutually exclusive. In fact, they cannot exist separately. For example, the defense cannot be purely passive resistance. An effective defense must assume an offensive character, striking at the moment of the enemy's greatest vulnerability. As Clausewitz wrote, the defense is "not a simple shield, but a shield made up of well-directed blows."[13] The truly decisive element of the defense is the counterattack. Thus, the offense is an integral component of the concept of the defense.

Similarly, the defense is an essential component of the offense. The offense cannot sustain itself indefinitely. At some times and places, it becomes necessary to halt the offense to replenish, and the defense automatically takes over. Furthermore, the requirement to concentrate forces for the offensive often necessitates assuming the defensive elsewhere. Therefore, out of necessity, we must include defensive considerations as part of our concept of the offense.

This brings us to the concept of the *culminating point*,[14] without which our understanding of the relationship between the offense and defense would be incomplete. Not only can the offense not sustain itself indefinitely, but also it generally grows weaker as it advances. Certain moral factors, such as morale or boldness, may increase with a successful attack, but these very often cannot compensate for the physical losses involved in sustaining an advance in the face of resistance. We advance at a cost in lives, fuel, ammunition, and physical and sometimes moral strength, and so the attack becomes weaker over time. Enemy resistance, of course, is a major factor in the dissipation of strength. Eventually, we reach the culminating point at which we can no longer sustain the attack and must revert to the defense. It is precisely at this point that the defensive element of the offense is most vulnerable to the offensive element of the defense, the counterattack.

We conclude that there exists no clear division between the offense and defense. Our theory of war should not attempt to impose one artificially. The offense and defense exist simultaneously as necessary components of each other, and the transition from one to the other is fluid and continuous.

These relationships between initiative and response, offense and defense, exist simultaneously at the various levels of war. We may seize the initiative locally as part of a larger response—in a limited counterattack, for example. Likewise, we may employ a tactical defense as part of an offensive campaign, availing ourselves of the advantages of the defense tactically while pursuing an operational offensive aim.

STYLES OF WARFARE

Styles in warfare can be described by their place on a spectrum of attrition and maneuver.[15] Warfare by attrition pursues victory through the cumulative destruction of the enemy's material assets by superior firepower. It is a direct approach to the conduct of war that sees war as a straightforward test of strength and a matter principally of force ratios. An enemy is seen as a collection of targets to be engaged and destroyed systematically. Enemy concentrations are sought out as the most worthwhile targets. The logical conclusion of attrition warfare is the eventual physical destruction of the enemy's entire arsenal, although the expectation is that the enemy will surrender or disengage before this happens out of unwillingness to bear the rising cost. The focus is on the efficient application of fires, leading to a highly proceduralized approach to war. Technical proficiency—especially in weapons employment—matters more than cunning or creativity.

Attrition warfare may recognize maneuver as an important component but sees its purpose as merely to allow us to bring our fires more efficiently to bear on the enemy. The attritionist tends to gauge progress in quantitative terms: battle damage assessments, "body counts," and terrain captured. Results are generally proportionate to efforts; greater expenditures net greater results—that is, greater attrition. The desire for volume and accuracy of fire tends to lead toward centralized control, just as the emphasis on efficiency tends to lead to an inward focus on procedures and techniques. Success depends on an overall superiority in attritional capacity—that is, the ability to inflict *and* absorb attrition. The greatest necessity for success is numerical and material superiority. At the national level, war becomes as much an industrial as a military problem. Historically, nations and militaries that perceived they were numerically and technologically superior have often adopted warfare by attrition.

Pure attrition warfare does not exist in practice, but examples of warfare with a high attrition content are plentiful: the operations of both sides on the Western Front of the First World War; the French defensive tactics and operations against the Germans in May 1940; the Allied campaign in Italy in 1943-1944; Eisenhower's broad-front offensive in Europe after Normandy in 1944; U.S. operations in Korea after 1950; and most U.S. operations in the Vietnam War.

On the opposite end of the spectrum is warfare by maneuver which stems from a desire to circumvent a problem and attack it from a position of advantage rather than meet it straight on. Rather than pursuing the cumulative destruction of every component in the enemy arsenal, the goal is to attack the enemy "system"—to incapacitate the enemy *systemically*. Enemy components may remain untouched but cannot function as part of a cohesive whole. Rather than being viewed as desirable targets, enemy concentrations are generally avoided as enemy strengths. Instead of attacking enemy strength, the goal is the application of our strength against selected enemy weakness in order to maximize *advantage*. This tack requires the ability to identify and exploit such weakness. Success depends not so much on the efficient performance of procedures and techniques, but on understanding the specific characteristics of the enemy system. Maneuver relies on speed and surprise for without either we cannot concentrate strength against enemy weakness. Tempo is itself a weapon—often the most important. Success by maneuver—unlike attrition—is often disproportionate to the effort made. However, for exactly the same reasons, maneuver incompetently applied carries with it a greater chance for catastrophic failure. With attrition, potential losses tend to be proportionate to risks incurred.

Firepower and attrition are essential elements of warfare by maneuver. In fact, at the critical point, where strength has been focused against enemy vulnerability, attrition may be extreme and may involve the outright annihilation of enemy elements. Nonetheless, the object of such local attrition is not merely to contribute incrementally to the overall wearing down of the entire enemy force, but to eliminate a key element which incapacitates the enemy systemically.

Like attrition warfare, maneuver warfare does not exist in its theoretically pure form. Examples of warfare with a high enough maneuver content that they can be considered maneuver warfare include Allenby's decisive campaign against the Turks in Palestine in 1918; German *Blitzkrieg* operations of 1939-1941, most notably the invasion of France in 1940; the failed Allied landing at Anzio in 1944, which was an effort to avoid the attrition battles of the Italian theater; Patton's break-out from the Normandy beachhead in late 1944; MacArthur's Inchon campaign in 1950; and III Marine Amphibious Force's combined action program in Vietnam which attacked the Viet Cong by eliminating their essential popular support base through the pacification of rural villages.

All warfare involves both maneuver and attrition in some mix. The predominant style depends on a variety of factors, not least of which are our own capabilities and the nature of the enemy. Marine Corps doctrine today is based principally on warfare by maneuver, as we will see in the fourth chapter, "The Conduct of War."

COMBAT POWER

Combat power is the total destructive force we can bring to bear on our enemy at a given time.[16] Some factors in combat power are quite tangible and easily measured such as superior numbers, which Clausewitz called "the most common element in victory."[17] Some may be less easily measured such as the effects of maneuver, tempo, or surprise; the advantages conferred by geography or climate; the relative strengths of the offense and defense; or the relative merits of striking the enemy in the front, flanks, or rear. Some may be wholly intangible such as morale, fighting spirit, perseverance, or the effects of leadership.

It is not our intent to try to list or categorize all the various components of combat power, to index their relative values, or to describe their combinations and variations; each combination is unique and temporary. Nor is it even desirable to be able to do so, since this would lead us to a formulaic approach to war. Our intent is merely to make the point that combat power is the situationally dependent and unique product of a variety of physical, moral, and mental factors.

SPEED AND FOCUS

Of all the consistent patterns we can discern in war, there are two concepts of universal significance in generating combat power: *speed* and *focus*.

Speed is rapidity of action. It applies to both time and space. Speed over time is tempo—the consistent ability to operate quickly.[18] Speed over distance, or space, is the ability to move rapidly. Both forms are genuine sources of combat power. In other words, *speed is a weapon*. In war, it is relative speed that matters rather than absolute speed. Superior speed allows us to seize the initiative and dictate the terms of action, forcing the enemy to react to us. Speed provides security. It is a prerequisite for maneuver and for surprise. Moreover, speed is necessary in order to concentrate superior strength at the decisive time and place.

Since it is relative speed that matters, it follows that we should take all measures to improve our own speed while degrading our enemy's. However, experience shows that we cannot sustain a high rate of speed indefinitely. As a result, a pattern develops: fast, slow, fast again. A competitive rhythm develops in combat with each belligerent trying to generate speed when it is advantageous.

Focus is the convergence of *effects* in time and space on some objective. It is the generation of superior combat power at a particular time and place. Focus may achieve decisive local superiority for a numerically inferior force. The willingness to focus at the decisive place and time necessitates strict economy and the acceptance of risk elsewhere and at other times. To devote means to unnecessary efforts or excessive means to necessary secondary efforts violates the principle of focus and is counterproductive to the true objective. Focus applies not only to the conduct of war but also to the preparation for war.

Since war is fluid and opportunities are fleeting, focus applies to time as well as to space. We must focus effects not only at the decisive location but also at the decisive moment.

We achieve focus through cooperation toward the accomplishment of the common purpose. This applies to all elements of the force, and involves the coordination of ground combat, aviation, and combat service support elements.

The combination of speed and focus adds "punch" or "shock effect" to our actions. It follows that we should strike with the greatest possible combination of speed and focus.

SURPRISE AND BOLDNESS

Two additional concepts are particularly useful in generating combat power: *surprise* and *boldness*.

By surprise we mean a state of disorientation resulting from an unexpected event that degrades the enemy's ability to resist. We achieve surprise by striking the enemy at a time or place or in a manner for which the enemy is unprepared. It is not essential that we take the enemy unaware, but only that awareness came too late to react effectively. The desire for surprise is "more or less basic to all operations, for without it superiority at the decisive point is hardly conceivable."[19] While a necessary precondition of superiority, surprise is also a genuine source of combat power in its own right because of its psychological effect. Surprise can decisively affect the outcome of combat far beyond the physical means at hand.

The advantage gained by surprise depends on the degree of disorientation and the enemy's ability to adjust and recover. Surprise, if sufficiently harsh, can lead to shock, the total, if temporary, inability to react. Surprise is based on speed, stealth, ambiguity, and deception. It often means doing the more difficult thing—taking a circuitous direction of attack, for example—in the hope that the enemy will not expect it. In fact, this is the genesis of maneuver—to circumvent the enemy's strength to strike at a weakness.

While the element of surprise is often of decisive importance, we must realize that it is difficult to achieve and easy to lose. Its advantages are only temporary and must be quickly exploited. Friction, a dominant attribute of war, is the constant enemy of surprise. We must also recognize that while surprise is always desirable, the ability to achieve it does not depend solely on our own efforts. Surprise is not what we *do*; it is the enemy's *reaction* to what we do. It depends at least as much on our enemy's susceptibility to surprise—his expectations and preparedness. Our ability to achieve surprise thus rests on our ability to appreciate and then exploit our enemy's expectations. Therefore, while surprise can be decisive, it is risky to depend on it alone for the margin of victory.

There are three basic ways to go about achieving surprise. The first is through *deception*—to convince the enemy we are going to do something other than what we are really going to do in order to induce him to act in a manner prejudicial to his own interests. The intent is to give the enemy a clear picture of the situation, but the wrong picture. The second way is through *ambiguity*—to act in such a way that the enemy does not know what to expect. Because he does not know what to expect, he must prepare for numerous possibilities and cannot prepare adequately for any one. The third is through *stealth*— to deny the enemy any knowledge of impending action. The enemy is not deceived or confused as to our intentions but is completely ignorant of them. Of the three, deception generally offers the greatest effects but is most difficult to achieve.

Boldness is a source of combat power in much the same way that surprise is. Boldness is the characteristic of unhes- itatingly exploiting the natural uncertainty of war to pursue major results rather than marginal ones. According to Clausewitz, boldness "must be granted a certain power over and above successful calculations involving space, time, and magnitude of forces, for wherever it is superior, it will take advantage of its opponent's weakness. In other words, it is a genuinely creative force."[20] Boldness is superior to timidity in every instance although boldness does not always equate to immediate aggressive action. A nervy, calculating patience that allows the enemy to commit himself irrevocably before we strike him can also be a form of boldness. Boldness is based on strong situation awareness: We weigh the situation, then act. In other words, boldness must be tempered with judgment lest it border on recklessness.

There is a close connection between surprise and boldness. The willingness to accept risks often necessary to achieve surprise reflects boldness. Likewise, boldness contributes to achieving surprise. After we weigh the situation, to take half measures diminishes the effects of surprise.

CENTERS OF GRAVITY AND CRITICAL VULNERABILITIES

It is not enough simply to generate superior combat power. We can easily conceive of superior combat power dissipated over several unrelated efforts or concentrated on some inconsequential object. To win, we must focus combat power toward a decisive aim. There are two related concepts that help us to think about this: *centers of gravity* and *critical vulnerabilities*.

Each belligerent is not a unitary force, but a complex system consisting of numerous physical, moral, and mental components as well as the relationships among them. The combination of these factors determines each belligerent's unique character. Some of these factors are more important than others. Some may contribute only marginally to the belligerent's power, and their loss would not cause significant damage. Others may be fundamental sources of capability.

We ask ourselves: *Which factors are critical to the enemy? Which can the enemy not do without? Which, if eliminated, will bend him most quickly to our will?* These are *centers of gravity.*[21] Depending on the situation, centers of gravity may be intangible characteristics such as resolve or morale. They may be capabilities such as armored forces or aviation strength. They may be localities such as a critical piece of terrain that anchors an entire defensive system. They may be the relationship between two or more components of the system such as the cooperation between two arms, the relations in an alliance, or the junction of two forces. In short, centers of gravity are any important sources of strength. If they are friendly centers of gravity, we want to protect them, and if they are enemy centers of gravity, we want to take them away.

We want to attack the source of enemy strength, but we do not want to attack directly into that strength. We obviously stand a better chance of success by concentrating our strength against some relative enemy weakness. So we also ask ourselves: *Where is the enemy vulnerable?* In battlefield terms, this means that we should generally avoid his front, where his attention is focused and he is strongest, and seek out his flanks and rear, where he does not expect us and where we can also cause the greatest psychological damage. We should also strike at a moment in time when he is vulnerable.

Of all the vulnerabilities we might choose to exploit, some are more critical to the enemy than others. Some may contribute significantly to the enemy's downfall while others may lead only to minimal gains. Therefore, we should focus our efforts against a *critical vulnerability*, a vulnerability that, if exploited, will do the most significant damage to the enemy's ability to resist us.

We should try to understand the enemy system in terms of a relatively few centers of gravity or critical vulnerabilities because this allows us to focus our own efforts. The more we can narrow it down, the more easily we can focus. However, we should recognize that most enemy systems will not have a single center of gravity on which everything else depends, or if they do, that center of gravity will be well protected. It will often be necessary to attack several lesser centers of gravity or critical vulnerabilities simultaneously or in sequence to have the desired effect.

Center of gravity and critical vulnerability are complementary concepts. The former looks at the problem of how to attack the enemy system from the perspective of seeking a source of strength, the latter from the perspective of seeking weakness. A critical vulnerability is a pathway to attacking a center of gravity. Both have the same underlying purpose: to target our actions in such a way as to have the greatest effect on the enemy.

CREATING AND EXPLOITING OPPORTUNITY

This discussion leads us to a corollary thought: the importance of creating and exploiting opportunity. In all cases, the commander must be prepared to react to the unexpected and to exploit opportunities created by conditions which develop from the initial action. When identification of enemy critical vulnerabilities is particularly difficult, the commander may have no choice but to exploit any and all vulnerabilities until action uncovers a decisive opportunity. As the opposing wills interact, they create various fleeting opportunities for either foe. Such opportunities are often born of the fog and friction that is natural in war. They may be the result of our own actions, enemy mistakes, or even chance. By exploiting opportunities, we create in increasing numbers more opportunities for exploitation. It is often the ability and the willingness to ruthlessly exploit these opportunities that generate decisive results. The ability to take advantage of opportunity is a function of speed, flexibility, boldness, and initiative.

CONCLUSION

The theory of war we have described provides the foundation for the discussion of the conduct of war in the final chapter. All acts of war are political acts, and so the conduct of war must be made to support the aims of policy. War takes place at several levels simultaneously, from the strategic direction of the overall war effort to the tactical application of combat power in battle. At the highest level, war involves the use of all the elements of political power, of which military force is just one. Action in war, at all levels, is the result of the interplay between initiative and response with the object being to seize and maintain the initiative. All warfare is based on concepts such as speed, focus, surprise, and boldness. Success in war depends on the ability to direct our efforts against criti- cal vulnerabilities or centers of gravity and to recognize and exploit fleeting opportunities. As we will discuss, the warfighting doctrine we derive from our theory is one based on maneuver.

Chapter 3

Preparing for War

"The essential thing is action. Action has three stages: the decision born of thought, the order or preparation for execution, and the execution itself. All three stages are governed by the will. The will is rooted in character, and for the man of action character is of more critical importance than intellect. Intellect without will is worthless, will without intellect is dangerous."[1]

—Hans von Seeck

"It is not enough that the troops be skilled infantry men or artillery men of high morale: they must be skilled water men and jungle men who know it can be done—Marines with Marine training."[2]

—Earl H. Ell

During times of peace, the most important task of any military is to prepare for war. Through its preparedness, a military provides deterrence against potential aggressors. As the nation's expeditionary force-in-readiness, the Marine Corps must maintain itself for immediate employment in "any clime and place" and in any type of conflict. All peacetime activities should focus on achieving combat readiness. This implies a high level of training, flexibility in organization and equipment, professional leadership, and a cohesive doctrine.

FORCE PLANNING

Force planning is planning that is associated with the creation and maintenance of military capabilities.[3] Planning plays as important a role in the preparation for war as it does in the conduct of war. The key to any plan is a clearly defined objective, in this case a required level of readiness.

The Marine Corps' force planning is concept-based. That is, all force planning derives from a common set of concepts which describe how Marine Corps forces will operate and perform certain key functions. These concepts describe the types of missions Marine forces are likely to be required to perform and how they might accomplish those missions. These concepts provide the basis for identifying required ca- pabilities and implementing coordinated programs to develop those capabilities.

Based on this common set of concepts, force planning integrates all the efforts of the peacetime Marine Corps, including training, education, doctrine, organization, personnel management, and equipment acquisition. Unity of effort is as important during the preparation for war as it is during the conduct of war. This systematic process of identifying the objective and planning a course to obtain it applies to all areas and levels of preparations.

ORGANIZATION

The operating forces must be organized to provide forward deployed or rapidly deployable forces capable of conducting expeditionary operations in any environment. This means that in addition to maintaining their unique amphibious capability, the operating forces must maintain the capability to deploy by whatever means is appropriate to the situation.

The active operating forces must be capable of responding immediately to most types of crisis and conflict. Many sustained missions will require augmentation from the Reserve establishment.

For operations and training, Marine forces will be formed into Marine air-ground task forces (MAGTFs). MAGTFs are task organizations consisting of ground, aviation, combat service support, and command elements. They have no standard structure, but rather are constituted as appropriate for the specific situation. The MAGTF provides a single commander a combined arms force that can be tailored to the situation faced. As the situation changes, it may of course be necessary to restructure the MAGTF.

Operating forces should be organized for warfighting and then adapted for peacetime rather than vice versa. Tables of organization should reflect the two central requirements of *deployability* and the *ability to task-organize according to specific situations*. Units should be organized according to type only to the extent dictated by training, administrative, and logistic requirements.

Commanders should establish habitual relationships between supported and supporting units to develop operational familiarity among those units. This does not preclude nonstandard relationships when required by the situation.

DOCTRINE

Doctrine is a teaching of the fundamental beliefs of the Marine Corps on the subject of war, from its nature and theory to its preparation and conduct.[4] Doctrine establishes a particular way of thinking about war and a way of fighting. It also provides a philosophy for leading Marines in combat, a mandate for professionalism, and a common language. In short, it establishes the way we practice our profession. In this manner, doctrine provides the basis for harmonious actions and mutual understanding.

Marine Corps doctrine is made official by the Commandant and is established in this publication. Our doctrine does not consist of procedures to be applied in specific situations so much as it sets forth general guidance that requires judgment in application. Therefore, while authoritative, doctrine is not prescriptive.

PROFESSIONALISM

Marine Corps doctrine demands professional competence among its leaders. *As military professionals charged with the defense of the Nation, Marine leaders must be true experts in the conduct of war.* They must be individuals both of action and of intellect, skilled at "getting things done" while at the same time conversant in the military art. Resolute and self-reliant in their decisions, they must also be energetic and insistent in execution.[5]

The military profession is a thinking profession. Ever Marine is expected to be a student of the art and science of war. Officers especially are expected to have a solid foundatio in military theory and a knowledge of military history and th timeless lessons to be gained from it.

Leaders must have a strong sense of the great responsibilit of their office; the resources they will expend in war are huma lives.

The Marine Corps' style of warfare requires intelligent leac ers with a penchant for boldness and initiative down to the low est levels. Boldness is an essential moral trait in a leader for generates combat power beyond the physical means at han Initiative, the willingness to act on one's own judgment, is prerequisite for boldness. These traits carried to excess ca lead to rashness, but we must realize that errors by junior lead ers stemming from overboldness are a necessary part o learning.[6] We should deal with such errors leniently; there mu be no "zero defects" mentality. Abolishing "zero defects means that we do not stifle boldness or initiative through th threat of punishment. It does not mean that commanders do nc counsel subordinates on mistakes; constructive criticism is a important element in learning. Nor does it give subordinate free license to act stupidly or recklessly.

Not only must we not stifle boldness or initiative, but w must continue to encourage both traits *in spite of mistakes*. O the other hand, we should deal severely with errors of inactio or timidity. We will not accept lack of orders as justification for inaction; it is each Marine's *duty* to take initiative as the situation demands. We must not tolerate the avoidance of responsibility or necessary risk.

Consequently, trust is an essential trait among leaders—trust by seniors in the abilities of their subordinates and by juniors in the competence and support of their seniors. Trust must be earned, and actions which undermine trust must meet with strict censure. Trust is a product of confidence and familiarity. Confidence among comrades results from demonstrated professional skill. Familiarity results from shared experience and a common professional philosophy.

Relations among all leaders—from corporal to general—should be based on honesty and frankness regardless of disparity between grades. Until a commander has reached and stated a decision, subordinates should consider it their duty to provide honest, professional opinions even though these may be in disagreement with the senior's opinions. However, once the decision has been reached, juniors then must support it as if it were their own. Seniors must encourage candor among subordinates and must not hide behind their grade insignia. Ready compliance for the purpose of personal advance- ment—the behavior of "yes-men"—will not be tolerated.

TRAINING

The purpose of all training is to develop forces that can win in combat. Training is the key to combat effectiveness and therefore is the main effort of a peacetime military. However, training should not stop with the commencement of war; training must continue during war to adapt to the lessons of combat.

All officers and enlisted Marines undergo similar entry-level training which is, in effect, a socialization process. This training provides all Marines a common experience, a proud heritage, a set of values, and a common bond of comradeship. It is the essential first step in the making of a Marine.

Basic individual skills are an essential foundation for combat effectiveness and must receive heavy emphasis. All Marines, regardless of occupational specialty, will be trained in basic combat skills. At the same time, unit skills are extremely important. They are not simply an accumulation of individual skills; adequacy in individual skills does not automatically mean unit skills are satisfactory.

Commanders at each echelon must allot subordinates sufficient time and freedom to conduct the training necessary to achieve proficiency at their levels. They must ensure that higher-level demands do not deny subordinates adequate opportunities for autonomous unit training.

In order to develop initiative among junior leaders, the conduct of training—like combat—should be decentralized. Senior commanders influence training by establishing goals and standards, communicating the intent of training, and establishing a main effort for training. As a rule, they should refrain from dictating how the training will be accomplished.

Training programs should reflect practical, challenging, and progressive goals beginning with individual and small-unit skills and culminating in a fully combined arms MAGTF. In general, the organization for combat should also be the organization for training. That is, units, including MAGTFs, should train with the full complement of assigned, reinforcing, and supporting forces they require in combat.

Collective training consists of drills and exercises. Drills are a form of small-unit training which stress proficiency by progressive repetition of tasks. Drills are an effective method for developing standardized techniques and procedures that must be performed repeatedly without variation to ensure speed and coordination. Examples are gun drills, preflight preparations, or immediate actions. In contrast, exercises are designed to train units and individuals in tactics under simulated combat conditions. Exercises should approximate the conditions of war as much as possible; that is, they should introduce friction in the form of uncertainty, stress, disorder, and opposing wills.

This last characteristic is most important; only in opposed free-play exercises can we practice the art of war. Dictated or "canned" scenarios eliminate the element of independent, opposing wills that is the essence of war.

Critiques are an important part of training because critical self-analysis, even after success, is essential to improvement. Their purpose is to draw out the lessons of training. As a result, we should conduct critiques immediately after completing training, before memory of the events has faded. Critiques should be held in an atmosphere of open and frank dialogue in which all hands are encouraged to contribute. We learn as much from mistakes as from things done well, so we must be willing to admit mistakes and discuss them. Of course, a subordinate's willingness to admit mistakes depends on the commander's willingness to tolerate them. Because we recognize that no two situations in war are the same, our critiques should focus not so much on the actions we took as on why we took those actions and why they brought the results they did.

PROFESSIONAL MILITARY EDUCATION

Professional military education is designed to develop creative thinking leaders. From the initial stages of leadership training, a leader's career should be viewed as a continuous, progressive process of development. At each stage, a Marine should be preparing for the subsequent stage.

The early stages of a leader's career are, in effect, an apprenticeship. While receiving a foundation in theory and concepts that will serve them throughout their careers, leaders focus on understanding the requirements and learning and applying the procedures and techniques associated with a particular field. This is when they learn their trades as aviators, infantrymen, artillerymen, or logisticians. As they progress, leaders should strive to master their respective fields and to understand the interrelationship of the techniques and procedures within the field. A Marine's goal at this stage is to become an expert in the tactical level of war.

As an officer continues to develop, mastery should encompass a broader range of subjects and should extend to the operational level of war. At this stage, an officer should not only be an expert in tactics and techniques but should also understand combined arms, amphibious warfare, and expeditionary operations. At the senior levels, an officer should be fully capable of articulating, applying, and integrating MAGTF warfighting capabilities in a joint and multinational environment and should be an expert in the art of war at all levels.

The responsibility for implementing professional military education in the Marine Corps is three-tiered: It resides not only with the education establishment, but also with the commander and the individual.

The education establishment consists of those schools— ad
ministered by the Marine Corps, subordinate commands, o
outside agencies—established to provide formal education i
the art and science of war. All professional schools, particu
larly officer schools, should focus on developing a talent fo
military judgment, not on imparting knowledge through rot
learning. Study conducted by the education establishment ca
neither provide complete career preparation for an individua
nor reach all individuals. Rather, it builds upon the base pro
vided by commanders and by individual study.

All commanders should consider the professional develop
ment of their subordinates a principal responsibility of com
mand. Commanders should foster a personal teacher-studen
relationship with their subordinates. Commanders are expecte
to conduct a continuing professional education program fo
their subordinates that includes developing military judgmen
and decisionmaking and teaches general professional subjec
and specific technical subjects pertinent to occupational spe
cialties. Useful tools for general professional development in
clude supervised reading programs, map exer- cises, wa
games, battle studies, and terrain studies. *Commanders shoul*
see the development of their subordinates as a direct refle
tion on themselves.

Finally, every Marine has an individual responsibility t
study the profession of arms. A leader without either interest i
or knowledge of the history and theory of warfare—the inte

ectual content of the military profession—is a leader in appearance only. Self-directed study in the art and science of war is at least equal in importance to maintaining physical condition and should receive at least equal time. This is particularly true among officers; after all, the mind is an officer's principal weapon.

PERSONNEL MANAGEMENT

Since war is at base a human enterprise, effective personnel management is important to success. This is especially true for a doctrine of maneuver warfare, which places a premium on individual judgment and action. We should recognize that all Marines of a given grade and occupational specialty are not interchangeable and should assign people to billets based on specific ability and temperament. This includes recognizing those who are best suited to command assignments and those who are best suited to staff assignments—without penalizing one or the other by so recognizing.

The personnel management system should seek to achieve personnel stability within units and staffs as a means of fostering cohesion, teamwork, and implicit understanding. We recognize that casualties in war will take a toll on personnel stability, but the greater stability a unit has initially, the better it will absorb those casualties and incorporate replacements.

Finally, promotion and advancement policy should reward the willingness to accept responsibility and exercise initiative.

EQUIPPING

Equipment should be easy to operate and maintain, reliable, and interoperable with other equipment. It should require minimal specialized operator training. Further, equipment should be designed so that its use is consistent with established doctrine and tactics. A primary consideration is strategic and tactical lift—the Marine Corps' reliance on shipping for strategic mobility and on landing craft, helicopters, and vertical/short takeoff and landing aircraft for tactical mobility from ship to shore and during operations ashore. Another key consideration is employability and supportability in undeveloped theaters with limited supporting infrastructure—where Marine Corps units can frequently expect to operate.

In order to minimize research and development costs and fielding time, the Marine Corps will exploit existing capabilities—"off-the-shelf" technology—to the greatest extent possible.

Acquisition should be a complementary, two-way process based on established operating and functional concepts. Especially for the long term, the process must identify combat requirements and develop equipment to satisfy these require-

ments. Where possible, we should base these requirements on
an analysis of likely enemy vulnerabilities and should develop
equipment to exploit those vulnerabilities. At the same time,
the process should not overlook existing equipment of obvious
usefulness.

Equipment is useful only if it increases combat effectiveness. Any piece of equipment requires support: operator training, maintenance, power sources or fuel, and transport. The
anticipated enhancement of capabilities must justify these support requirements and the employment of the equipment must
take these requirements into account.

The acquisition effort should balance the need for speciali-
zation with the need for utility in a broad range of environ-
ments. Increasing the capabilities of equipment generally
requires developing increasingly specialized equipment. Increasingly specialized equipment tends to be increasingly vulnerable to countermeasures. One solution to this problem is not
to develop a single family of equipment, but to maintain variety
in equipment types.

As much as possible, employment techniques and procedures should be developed concurrently with equipment to
minimize delays between the fielding of the equipment and its
usefulness to the operating forces. For the same reason, initial
operator training should also precede equipment fielding.

There are two dangers with respect to equipment: the overreliance on technology and the failure to make the most of technological capabilities. Technology can enhance the way and means of war by improving humanity's ability to wage it but technology cannot and should not attempt to eliminate humanity from the process of waging war. Better equipment is not the cure for all ills; doctrinal and tactical solutions to combat deficiencies must also be sought. Any advantages gained by technological advancement are only temporary for someone will always find a countermeasure, tactical or itself technological, which will lessen the impact of the technology. Additionally, we must not become so dependent on equipment that we can no longer function effectively when the equipment becomes inoperable. Finally, we must exercise discipline in the use of technology. Advanced information technology especially can tempt us to try to maintain precise, positive control over subordinates, which is incompatible with the Marine Corps philosophy of command.

CONCLUSION

There are two basic military functions: waging war and preparing for war. Any military activities that do not contribute to the conduct of a present war are justifiable only if they contribute to preparedness for a possible future one. Clearly, we cannot afford to separate conduct and preparation. They must be intiately related because failure in preparation leads to disaster on the battlefield.

Chapter 4

The Conduct of War

"Now an army may be likened to water, for just as flowing water avoids the heights and hastens to the lowlands, so an army avoids strength and strikes weakness."[1]

—Sun Tzu

"Speed is the essence of war. Take advantage of the enemy's unpreparedness; travel by unexpected routes and strike him where he has taken no precautions."[2]

—Sun Tzu

"Many years ago, as a cadet hoping some day to be an officer, I was poring over the 'Principles of War,' listed in the old Field Service Regulations, when the Sergeant-Major came up to me. He surveyed me with kindly amusement. 'Don't bother your head about all them things, me lad,' he said. 'There's only one principle of war and that's this. Hit the other fellow, as quick as you can, and as hard as you can, where it hurts him most, when he ain't lookin'!'"[3]

—Sir William Slim

T he sole justification for the United States Marine Corps is to secure or protect national policy objectives by military force when peaceful means alone cannot. How the Marine Corps proposes to accomplish this mission is the product of our understanding of the nature and the theory of war and must be the guiding force behind our preparation for war.

THE CHALLENGE

The challenge is to develop a concept of warfighting consistent with our understanding of the nature and theory of war and the realities of the modern battlefield. What exactly does this require? It requires a concept of warfighting that will help us function effectively in an uncertain, chaotic, and fluid environment—in fact, one with which we can exploit these conditions to our advantage. It requires a concept with which we can sense and use the time-competitive rhythm of war to generate and exploit superior tempo. It requires a concept that is consistently effective across the full spectrum of conflict because we cannot attempt to change our basic doctrine from situation to situation and expect to be proficient. It requires a concept with which we can recognize and exploit the fleeting opportunities that naturally occur in war. It requires a concept that takes into account the moral and mental as well as the physical forces of war because we have already concluded that these form the greater part of war. It requires a concept with which we can succeed against a numerically superior foe because we cannot presume a numerical advantage either locally or overall. Especially in expeditionary situations in which public support for military action may be tepid and short-lived, it requires a concept with which we can win quickly against a larger foe on his home soil with minimal casualties and limited external support.

MANEUVER WARFARE

The Marine Corps concept for winning under these conditions is a warfighting doctrine based on rapid, flexible, and opportunistic maneuver. In order to fully appreciate what we mean by *maneuver*, we need to clarify the term. The traditional understanding of maneuver is a spatial one; that is, we maneuver in space to gain a positional advantage.[4] However, in order to maximize the usefulness of maneuver, we must consider maneuver in other dimensions as well. The essence of maneuver is taking action to generate and exploit some kind of advantage over the enemy as a means of accomplishing our objectives as effectively as possible. That advantage may be psychological, technological, or temporal as well as spatial. Especially important is maneuver *in time*—we generate a faster operating tempo than the enemy to gain a temporal advantage. It is through maneuver in all dimensions that an inferior force can achieve decisive superiority at the necessary time and place.

Maneuver warfare is a warfighting philosophy that seeks t *shatter the enemy's cohesion through a variety of rapid, fo-* *cused, and unexpected actions which create a turbulent an* *rapidly deteriorating situation with which the enemy canno* *cope.*

Rather than wearing down an enemy's defenses, maneuve warfare attempts to bypass these defenses in order to *penetrate* the enemy system and tear it apart. The aim is to render the en- emy incapable of resisting effectively by shattering his moral mental, and physical cohesion—his ability to fight as an effec tive, coordinated whole—rather than to destroy him physicall through the incremental attrition of each of his components which is generally more costly and time-con- suming. Ideally the components of his physical strength that remain are irrele vant because we have disrupted his ability to use them effec tively. Even if an outmaneuvered enemy continues to fight a individuals or small units, we can destroy the remnants witl relative ease because we have eliminated his ability to fight ef fectively as a force.

This is not to imply that firepower is unimportant. On the contrary, firepower is central to maneuver warfare. Nor do we mean to imply that we will pass up the opportunity to physi cally destroy the enemy. We will concentrate fires and forces a decisive points to destroy enemy elements when the oppor tunity presents itself and when it fits our larger purposes. En- gaged in combat, we can rarely go wrong if we aggressivel pursue the destruction of enemy forces. In fact, maneuver warfare often involves extremely high attrition of selected enemy forces where we have focused combat power against critical enemy weakness. Nonetheless, the aim of such attrition is not merely to reduce incrementally the enemy's physical strength. Rather, it is to contribute to the enemy's systemic disruption. The greatest effect of firepower is gen- erally not physical destruction—the cumulative effects of which are felt only slowly—but the disruption it causes.

If the aim of maneuver warfare is to shatter the cohesion of the enemy system, the immediate object toward that end is to create a situation in which the enemy cannot function. By our actions, we seek to pose menacing dilemmas in which events happen unexpectedly and more quickly than the enemy can keep up with them. The enemy must be made to see the situation not only as deteriorating, but deteriorating at an ever-increasing rate. The ultimate goal is panic and paralysis, an enemy who has lost the ability to resist.

Inherent in maneuver warfare is the need for *speed* to seize the initiative, dictate the terms of action, and keep the enemy off balance, thereby increasing his friction. We seek to establish a pace that the enemy cannot maintain so that with each action his reactions are increasingly late—until eventually he is overcome by events.

Also inherent is the need to *focus* our efforts in order to maximize effect. In combat this includes violence and shock effect, again not so much as a source of physical attrition, but as

a source of disruption. We concentrate strength against critica
enemy vulnerabilities, striking quickly and boldly where, whe
and in ways in which it will cause the greatest damage to o
enemy's ability to fight. Once gained or found, any advantag
must be pressed relentlessly and unhesitatingly. We must b
ruthlessly opportunistic, actively seeking out signs of weaknes
against which we will direct all available combat power. Whe
the *decisive* opportunity arrives, we must exploit it fully an
aggressively, committing every ounce of combat power we ca
muster and pushing ourselves to the limits of exhaustion.

An important weapon in our arsenal is *surprise*, the com
bat value of which we have already recognized. By studyin
our enemy, we will attempt to appreciate his perception:
Through deception we will try to shape the enemy's expecta
tions. Then we will exploit those expectations by striking at a
unexpected time and place. In order to appear unpredictabl
we must avoid set rules and patterns, which inhibit imaginatio
and initiative. In order to appear ambiguous and threatenin
we should operate on axes that offer numerous courses of a
tion, keeping the enemy unclear as to which we will choose.

Besides traits such as endurance and courage that all wa
fare demands, maneuver warfare puts a premium on certai
particular human skills and traits. It requires the temperamen
to cope with uncertainty. It requires flexibility of mind to de
with fluid and disorderly situations. It requires a certain inde
pendence of mind, a willingness to act with initiative and bold
ness, an exploitive mindset that takes full advantage of ever

opportunity, and the moral courage to accept responsibility for his type of behavior. It is important that this last set of traits be guided by self-discipline and loyalty to the objectives of seniors. Finally, maneuver warfare requires the ability to think above our own level and to act at our level in a way that is in consonance with the requirements of the larger situation.

ORIENTING ON THE ENEMY

Orienting on the enemy is fundamental to maneuver warfare. Maneuver warfare attacks the enemy "system." The enemy system is whatever constitutes the entity confronting us within our particular sphere. For a pilot, it might be the combination of air defense radars, surface-to-air missiles, and enemy aircraft that must be penetrated to reach the target. For a rifle company commander, it might be the mutually supporting defensive positions, protected by obstacles and supported by crew-served weapons, on the next terrain feature. For an electronic warfare specialist, it might be the enemy's command and control networks. For a Marine expeditionary force commander, it might be all the major combat formations within an area of operations as well as their supporting command and control, logistics, and intelligence organizations.

We should try to understand the unique characteristics that make the enemy system function so that we can penetrate the system, tear it apart, and, if necessary, destroy the isolated components. We should seek to identify and attack critical vulnerabilities and those centers of gravity without which the enemy cannot function effectively. This means focusing outward on the particular characteristics of the enemy rather than inward on the mechanical execution of predetermined procedures.

If the enemy system, for example, is a fortified defensive works, penetrating the system may mean an infiltration or a violent attack on a narrow frontage at a weak spot to physically rupture the defense, after which we can envelop the enemy positions or roll them up laterally from within. In this way we defeat the logic of the system rather than frontally overwhelming each position.

We should try to "get inside" the enemy's thought processes and see the enemy as he sees himself so that we can set him up for defeat. It is essential that we understand the enemy on his own terms. We should not assume that every enemy thinks as we do, fights as we do, or has the same values or objectives.

PHILOSOPHY OF COMMAND

It is essential that our philosophy of command support the way we fight. First and foremost, *in order to generate the tempo of operations we desire and to best cope with the uncertainty, disorder, and fluidity of combat, command and control must e decentralized*. That is, subordinate commanders must make decisions on their own initiative, based on their understanding of their senior's intent, rather than passing information up the chain of command and waiting for the decision to be passed down. Further, a competent subordinate commander who is at the point of decision will naturally better appreciate the true situation than a senior commander some distance removed. Individual initiative and responsibility are of paramount importance. The principal means by which we implement decentralized command and control is through the use of mission tactics, which we will discuss in detail later.

Second, since we have concluded that war is a human enterprise and no amount of technology can reduce the human dimension, our philosophy of command must be based on human characteristics rather than on equipment or procedures. Communications equipment and command and staff procedures can enhance our ability to command, but they must not be used to lessen the human element of command. Our philosophy must not only accommodate but must exploit human traits such as boldness, initiative, personality, strength of will, and imagination.

Our philosophy of command must also exploit the human ability to communicate *implicitly*.[5] We believe that *implicit communication*—to communicate through *mutual understanding*, using a minimum of key, well-understood phrases or even *anticipating* each other's thoughts—is a faster, more effective way to communicate than through the use of detailed, explicit instructions. We develop this ability through familiarity and trust, which are based on a shared philosophy an shared experience.

This concept has several practical implications. First, we should establish long-term working relationships to develop the necessary familiarity and trust. Second, key people—"actual s"—should talk directly to one another when possible, rathe than through communicators or messengers. Third, we should communicate orally when possible, because we communicate also in *how* we talk—our inflections and tone of voice. Fourth we should communicate in person when possible because we communicate also through our gestures and bearing.

Commanders should command from where they can best in fluence the action, normally well forward. This allows them to see and sense firsthand the ebb and flow of combat, to gain at intuitive appreciation for the situation that they cannot obtain from reports. It allows them to exert personal influence at deci sive points during the action. It also allows them to locate themselves closer to the events that will influence the situation so that they can observe them directly and circumvent the de lays and inaccuracies that result from passing information up and down the chain of command. Finally, we recognize the im portance of personal leadership. Only by their physical pres ence—by demonstrating the willingness to share danger and privation—can commanders fully gain the trust and confidence of subordinates. *We must remember that command from the front should not equate to oversupervision of subordinates. A* the same time, it is important to balance the need for forward ommand with the need for keeping apprised of the overall situation, which is often best done from a central location such as a combat operation center. Commanders cannot become so focused on one aspect of the situation that they lose overall situational awareness.

As part of our philosophy of command, we must recognize that war is inherently disorderly, uncertain, dynamic, and dominated by friction. Moreover, maneuver warfare, with its emphasis on speed and initiative, is by nature a particularly disorderly style of war. The conditions ripe for exploitation are normally also very disorderly. For commanders to try to gain certainty as a basis for actions, maintain positive control of events at all times, or dictate events to fit their plans is to deny the nature of war. We must therefore be prepared to cope—even better, to *thrive*—in an environment of chaos, uncertainty, constant change, and friction. If we can come to terms with those conditions and thereby limit their debili- tating effects, we can use them as a weapon against a foe who does not cope as well.

In practical terms, this means that we must not strive for certainty before we act, for in so doing we will surrender the initiative and pass up opportunities. We must not try to main- tain excessive control over subordinates since this will neces- sarily slow our tempo and inhibit initiative. We must not attempt to impose precise order on the events of combat since this leads to a formularistic approach to war. We must be pre- pared to adapt to changing circumstances and exploit opportunities as they arise, rather than adhering insistently **t** predetermined plans that have outlived their usefulness.

There are several points worth remembering about our com mand philosophy. First, while it is based on our warfightin style, this does not mean it applies only during war. We mu put it into practice during the preparation for war as well. W cannot rightly expect our subordinates to exercise boldness an initiative in the field when they are accustomed to being ove supervised in garrison. Whether the mission is training, procu ing equipment, administration, or police call, this philosoph should apply.

Next, our philosophy requires competent leadership at a levels. A centralized system theoretically needs only one com petent person, the senior commander, who is the sole authorit A decentralized system requires leaders at all levels to demon strate sound and timely judgment. Initiative be- comes an es sential condition of competence among commanders.

Our philosophy also requires familiarity among comrade because only through a shared understanding can we develo the implicit communication necessary for unity of effort. Pe haps most important, our philosophy demands confidenc among seniors and subordinates.

SHAPING THE ACTION

Since our goal is not merely the cumulative attrition of enemy strength, we must have some larger scheme for how we expect to achieve victory. That is, before anything else, we must conceive how we intend to win.

The first requirement is to establish what we want to accomplish, why, and how. Without a clearly identified concept and intent, the necessary unity of effort is inconceivable. We must identify those *critical* enemy vulnerabilities that we believe will lead most directly to undermining the enemy's centers of gravity and the accomplishment of our mission. Having done this, we can then begin to act so as to shape the campaign, operation, battle, or engagement to our advantage in both time and space. Similarly, we must try to see ourselves through our enemy's eyes in order to identify our own vulnerabilities that he may attack and to anticipate what he will try to do so that we can counteract him. Ideally, when the moment of engagement arrives, the issue will have already been resolved: Through our influencing of the events leading up to the encounter, we have so shaped the conditions of war that the result is a matter of course. We have shaped the action decisively to our advantage.

To influence the action to our advantage, we must project our thoughts forward in time and space. We frequently do this through planning. This does not mean that we establish a detailed timetable of events. We have already concluded that war is inherently disorderly, and we cannot expect to dictate its terms with any sort of precision. Rather, we attempt to shape the general conditions of war. This shaping consists of lethal and nonlethal actions that span the spectrum from direct attack to psychological operations, from electronic warfare to the stockpiling of critical supplies for future operations. Shaping activities may render the enemy vulnerable to attack, facilitate maneuver of friendly forces, and dictate the time and place for decisive battle. Examples include canalizing enemy movement in a desired direction, blocking or delaying enemy reinforcements so that we can fight a fragmented enemy force, or shaping enemy expectations through deception so that we can exploit those expectations. We can attack a specific enemy capability to allow us to maximize a capability of our own such as launching an operation to destroy the enemy's air defenses so that we can maximize the use of our own aviation.

Through shaping, commanders gain the initiative, preserve momentum, and control the tempo of operations. We should also try to shape events in a way that allows us several options so that by the time the moment for decisive operations arrives, we have not restricted ourselves to only one course of action.

The further ahead we think, the less our actual influence can be. Therefore, the further ahead we consider, the less precision we should attempt to impose. Looking ahead thus becomes less a matter of direct influence and more a matter of laying the groundwork for possible future actions. As events approach

nd our ability to influence them grows, we have already devel-
ped an appreciation for the situation and how we want to
shape it.[6]

The higher our echelon of command, the greater is our
sphere of influence and the further ahead in time and space we
must seek to shape the action. Senior commanders developing
nd pursuing military strategy look ahead weeks, months, or
more, and their areas of influence and interest will encompass
entire theaters. Junior commanders fighting the battles and engagements at hand are concerned with the coming hours, even
minutes, and the immediate field of battle. Regardless of the
sphere in which we operate, it is essential to have some vision
f the result we want and how we intend to shape the action in
time and space to achieve it.

DECISIONMAKING

Decisionmaking is essential to the conduct of war since all ac-
ions are the result of decisions or of nondecisions. If we fail to
make a decision out of lack of will, we have willingly surren-
dered the initiative to our foe. If we consciously postpone tak-
ng action for some reason, that is a decision. Thus, as a basis
or action, any decision is generally better than no decision.

Since war is a conflict between opposing wills, we cannot
make decisions in a vacuum. We must make our decisions in

light of the enemy's anticipated reactions and counteractions, recognizing that while we are trying to impose our will on the enemy, he is trying to do the same to us.

Time is a critical factor in effective decisionmaking—often the most important factor. A key part of effective decisionmaking is realizing how much decision time is available and making the most of that time. In general, whoever can make and implement decisions consistently faster gains a tremendous, often decisive advantage. Decisionmaking in execution thus becomes a time-competitive process, and timeliness of decision becomes essential to generating tempo. Timely decisions demand rapid thinking with consideration limited to essential factors. In such situations, we should spare no effort to accelerate our decisionmaking ability. That said, we should also recognize those situations in which time is not a limiting factor—such as deliberate planning situations—and should not rush our decisions unnecessarily.

A military decision is not merely a mathematical computation. Decisionmaking requires both the situational awareness to recognize the essence of a given problem and the creative ability to devise a practical solution. These abilities are the products of experience, education, and intelligence.

Decisionmaking may be an intuitive process based on experience. This will likely be the case at lower levels and in fluid, uncertain situations. Alternatively, decisionmaking may be a more analytical process based on comparing several options.

his will more likely be the case at higher levels or in deliberate planning situations.

We should base our decisions on *awareness* rather than on mechanical *habit*. That is, we act on a keen appreciation for the essential factors that make each situation unique instead of from conditioned response. We must have the moral courage to make tough decisions in the face of uncertainty—and to accept full responsibility for those decisions—when the natural inclination would be to postpone the decision pending more complete information. To delay action in an emergency because of incomplete information shows a lack of moral courage. We do not want to make rash decisions, but we must not squander opportunities while trying to gain more information.

Finally, since all decisions must be made in the face of uncertainty and since every situation is unique, there is no perfect solution to any battlefield problem. Therefore, we should not agonize over one. The essence of the problem is to select a promising course of action with an acceptable degree of risk and to do it more quickly than our foe. In this respect, "a good plan violently executed *now* is better than a perfect plan executed next week."[7]

MISSION TACTICS

One key way we put maneuver warfare into practice is throug
the use of *mission tactics*. Mission tactics is just as the nam
implies: the tactics of assigning a subordinate mission withou
specifying how the mission must be accom- plished.[8] We leav
the manner of accomplishing the mission to the subordinat
thereby allowing the freedom—and establishing the duty—f
the subordinate to take whatever steps deemed necessary base
on the situation. Mission tactics relies on a subordinate's exer
cise of initiative framed by proper guidance and understanding

Mission tactics benefits the senior commander by freein
time to focus on higher-level concerns rather than the details c
subordinate execution. The senior prescribes the method c
execution only to the degree that is essential for coordination
The senior intervenes in a subordinate's execution only by ex
ception. It is this freedom for initiative that permits the hig
tempo of operations that we desire. Uninhibited by excessiv
restrictions from above, subordinates can adapt their actions t
the changing situation. They inform the commander of wha
they have done, but they do not wait for permission.

Mission tactics serves as a contract between senior and sut
ordinate. The senior agrees to provide subordinates with th
support necessary to help them accomplish their mis- sions bu
without unnecessarily prescribing their actions. The senior
obligated to provide the guidance that allows subor- dinates t

exercise proper judgment and initiative. The subor- dinate is obligated to act in conformity with the intent of the senior. The subordinate agrees to act responsibly and loyally and not to exceed the proper limits of authority. Mission tactics requires subordinates to act with "topsight"—a grasp of how their actions fit into the larger situation.[9] In other words, subordinates must always think above their own levels in order to contribute to the accomplishment of the higher mission.

It is obvious that we cannot allow decentralized initiative without some means of providing unity, or focus, to the various efforts. To do so would be to dissipate our strength. We seek unity not principally through imposed control, but through *harmonious* initiative and lateral coordination within the context provided by guidance from above.

COMMANDER'S INTENT

We achieve this harmonious initiative in large part through the use of the commander's *intent*, a device designed to help subordinates understand the larger context of their actions. The purpose of providing intent is to allow subordinates to exercise judgment and initiative—to depart from the original plan when the unforeseen occurs—in a way that is consistent with higher commanders' aims.

There are two parts to any *mission*: the task to be accomplished and the reason or intent behind it.[10] The intent is thus a part of every mission. The task describes the action to be taken while the intent describes the *purpose* of the action. The task denotes *what* is to be done, and sometimes *when* and *where*; the intent explains *why*. Of the two, the intent is predominant. While a situation may change, making the task obsolete, the intent is more lasting and continues to guide our actions. Understanding the intent of our commander allows us to exercise initiative in harmony with the commander's desires.

The intent for a unit is established by the commander assigning that unit's mission—usually the next higher commander, although not always. A commander normally provides intent as part of the mission statement assigned to a subordinate. A subordinate commander who is not given a clear purpose for the assigned mission should ask for one. Based on the mission, the commander then develops a concept of operations which explains *how* the unit will accomplish the mission, and assigns missions to subordinates. Each subordinate mission statement includes an intent for that subordinate. The intent provided to each subordinate should contribute to the accomplishment of the intent a commander has received from above. This top-down flow of intent provides consistency and continuity to our actions and establishes the context that is essential for the proper bottom-up exercise of initiative.

It is often possible to capture intent in a simple ". . . in order to . . ." phrase following the assigned task. To maintain our focus on the enemy, we can often express intent in terms of the enemy. For example: "Control the bridge in order to prevent the enemy from escaping across the river." Sometimes it may be necessary to provide amplifying guidance in addition to an ". . . in order to . . ." statement. In any event, a commander's statement of intent should be brief and compelling—the more concise, the better. A subordinate should be ever conscious of a senior's intent so that it guides every decision. An intent that is involved or complicated will fail to accomplish this purpose.

A clear expression and understanding of intent is essential to unity of effort. The burden of understanding falls on senior and subordinate alike. The seniors must make their purposes perfectly clear but in a way that does not inhibit initiative. Subordinates must have a clear understanding of what their commander expects. Further, they should understand the intent of the commander at least two levels up.

MAIN EFFORT

Another important tool for providing unity is the *main ef- fort*. Of all the actions going on within our command, we recognize one as the most critical to success at that moment. The *unit* assigned responsibility for accomplishing this key mission is designated as the main effort—the focal point upon which converges the combat power of the force. The main effort receives priority for support of any kind. It becomes clear to all other units in the command that they must support that unit in the accomplishment of its mission. Like the commander's in tent, the main effort becomes a harmonizing force for subordinate initiative. Faced with a decision, we ask ourselves: *How can I best support the main effort?*

We cannot take lightly the decision of which unit we desig nate as the main effort. In effect, we have decided: *This is how I will achieve a decision; everything else is secondary.* We carefully design the operation so that success by the main effort ensures the success of the entire mission. Since the main effort represents our primary bid for victory, we must direct it at that object which will have the most significant effect on the enemy and which holds the best opportunity of success. The main effort involves a physical and moral commitment, although not an irretrievable one. It forces us to concentrate deci sive combat power just as it forces us to accept risk. Thus, we direct our main effort against a center of gravity through a critical enemy vulnerability, exercising strict economy else where.

Each commander should establish a main effort for each op eration. As the situation changes, the commander may shift the main effort, redirecting the weight of combat power in suppor of the unit that is now most critical to success. In general when shifting the main effort, we seek to exploit success rathe than reinforce failure.

SURFACES AND GAPS

Put simply, surfaces are hard spots—enemy strengths—and gaps are soft spots—enemy weaknesses. We avoid enemy strength and focus our efforts against enemy weakness with the object of penetrating the enemy system since pitting strength against weakness reduces casualties and is more likely to yield decisive results. Whenever possible, we exploit existing gaps. Failing that, we create gaps.

Gaps may in fact be physical gaps in the enemy's dispositions, but they may also be any weakness in time, space, or capability: a moment in time when the enemy is overexposed and vulnerable, a seam in an air defense umbrella, an infantry unit caught unprepared in open terrain, or a boundary between two units.

Similarly, a surface may be an actual strongpoint, or it may be any enemy strength: a moment when the enemy has just replenished and consolidated a position or a technological superiority of a particular weapons system or capability.

An appreciation for surfaces and gaps requires a certain amount of judgment. What is a surface in one case may be a gap in another. For example, a forest which is a surface to an armored unit because it restricts vehicle movement can be a gap to an infantry unit which can infiltrate through it. Furthermore, we can expect the enemy to disguise his dispositions in order to lure us against a surface that appears to be a gap.

Due to the fluid nature of war, gaps will rarely be perma nent and will usually be fleeting. To exploit them demand flexibility and speed. We must actively seek out gaps by con tinuous and aggressive reconnaissance. Once we locate them we must exploit them by funneling our forces through rapidly For example, if our main effort has struck a surface but an other unit has located a gap, we designate the second unit a the main effort and redirect our combat power in support of it In this manner, we "pull" combat power through gaps from th front rather than "pushing" it through from the rear.[11] Com manders must rely on the initiative of subordinates to locat gaps and must have the flexibility to respond quick- ly to op portunities rather than blindly follow predetermined schemes.

COMBINED ARMS

In order to maximize combat power, we must use all the avail able resources to best advantage. To do so, we must follow doctrine of combined arms. Combined arms is the full integra tion of arms in such a way that to counteract one, the enem must become more vulnerable to another. We pose the enem not just with a problem, but with a dilemma—a no-win situa tion.

We accomplish combined arms through the tactics and techniques we use at the lower levels and through task organization at higher levels. In so doing, we take advantage of the complementary characteristics of different types of units and enhance our mobility and firepower. We use each arm for missions that no other arm can perform as well; for example, we assign aviation a task that cannot be performed equally well by artillery. An example of the concept of combined arms at the very lowest level is the complementary use of the automatic weapon and grenade launcher within a fire team. We pin an enemy down with the high-volume, direct fire of the automatic weapon, making him a vulnerable target for the grenade launcher. If he moves to escape the impact of the grenades, we engage him with the automatic weapon.

We can expand the example to the MAGTF level: We use assault support aircraft to quickly concentrate superior ground forces for a breakthrough. We use artillery and close air support to support the infantry penetration, and we use deep air support to interdict enemy reinforcements that move to contain the penetration. Targets which cannot be effectively suppressed by artillery are engaged by close air support. In order to defend against the infantry attack, the enemy must make himself vulnerable to the supporting arms. If he seeks cover from the supporting arms, our infantry can maneuver against him. In order to block our penetration, the enemy must reinforce quickly with his reserve. However, in order to avoid our deep air support, he must stay off the roads, which means he can only move slowly.

If he moves slowly, he cannot reinforce in time to prevent our breakthrough. We have put him in a dilemma.

CONCLUSION

We have discussed the aim and characteristics of maneuver warfare. We have discussed the philosophy of command necessary to support this style of warfare. We have discussed some of the tactics of maneuver warfare. By this time, it should be clear that maneuver warfare exists not so much in the specific methods used—we do not believe in a formularistic approach to war—but in the mind of the Marine. In this regard, maneuver warfare, like combined arms, applies equally to the Marine expeditionary force commander and the fire team leader. It applies regardless of the nature of the con- flict, whether amphibious operations or sustained operations ashore, of low or high intensity, against guerrilla or mechanized foe, in desert or jungle.

Maneuver warfare is a way of thinking in and about war that should shape our every action. It is a state of mind born of a bold will, intellect, initiative, and ruthless opportunism. It is a state of mind bent on shattering the enemy morally and physically by paralyzing and confounding him, by avoiding his strength, by quickly and aggressively exploiting his vulnerabilities, and by striking him in the way that will hurt him most. In short, maneuver warfare is a philosophy for generating the greatest decisive effect against the enemy at the least possible cost to ourselves—a philosophy for "fighting smart."

The Nature of War

1.   Carl von Clausewitz, *On War*, trans. and ed. Michael Howard and Peter Paret (Princeton, NJ: Princeton University Press 1984) p. 119. This unfinished classic is arguably the definitive treatment of the nature and theory of war. All Marine officers should consider this book essential reading.

2.   B. H. Liddell Hart, *Strategy* (New York: New American Library, 1974) p. 323.

3.   A. A. Vandegrift, *"Battle Doctrine for Front Line Leaders,"* (Third Marine Division, 1944) p. 7.

4.   "War is nothing but a duel [*Zweikampf*, literally 'two struggle'] on a larger scale. Countless duels go to make up war, but a picture of it as a whole can be formed by imagining a pair of wrestlers. Each tries through physical force to compel the other to do his will; his *immediate* aim is to *throw* his opponent in order to make him incapable of further resistance." Clausewitz, *On War*, p. 75. See also Alan Beyerchen, "Clausewitz, Nonlinearity, and the Unpredictability of War," *International Security* (Winter 1992/1993) pp. 66–67.

5.   Clausewitz, p. 121.

6.   Ibid., p. 595.

7. For a first-hand description of human experience and reaction in war, read Guy Sajer's *The Forgotten Soldier* (Baltimore, MD: Nautical and Aviation Publishing Co., 1988), a powerful account of the author's experience as a German infantryman on the eastern front during the Second World War.

8. "Kind-hearted people might, of course, think there was some ingenious way to disarm or defeat an enemy without too much bloodshed, and might imagine this is the true goal of the art of war. Pleasant as it sounds, it is a fallacy that must be exposed: war is such a dangerous business that the mistakes which come from kindness are the very worst . . .

"This is how the matter must be seen. It would be futile—even wrong—to try to shut one's eyes to what war really is from sheer distress at its brutality." Clausewitz, pp. 75–76.

9. For an insightful study of the reaction of men to combat, see S. L. A. Marshall's *Men Against Fire* (New York: William Morrow and Co., 1961). Despite criticism of his research methods, Marshall's insights on this point remain valuable.

10. *The American Heritage Dictionary* (New York: Dell Publishing Co., 1983).

11. In his often-quoted maxim, Napoleon assigned an actual ratio: "In war, the moral is to the material as three to one." Peter G. Tsouras, *Warrior's Words: A Dictionary of Military Quotations* (London: Cassell, 1992) p. 266.

The Theory of War

1. Clausewitz, p. 87.

2. Sun Tzu, *The Art of War*, trans. S. B. Griffith (New York: Oxford University Press, 1982) p. 85. Like *On War, The Art of War* should be on every Marine officer's list of essential reading. Short and simple to read, *The Art of War* is every bit as valuable today as when it was written about 400 B.C..

3. Winston S. Churchill, *The World Crisis,* vol. 2 (New York: Charles Scribner's Sons, 1923) p. 5. The passage continues: "Nearly all battles which are regarded as masterpieces of the military art, from which have been derived the foundation of states and the fame of commanders, have been battles of manoeuvre in which the enemy has found himself defeated by some novel expedient or device, some queer, swift, unexpected thrust or stratagem. In many battles the losses of the victors have been small. There is required for the composition of a great commander not only massive common sense and reasoning power, not only imagination, but also an element of legerdemain, an original and sinister touch, which leaves the enemy puzzled as well as beaten. It is because military leaders are credited with gifts of this order which enable them to ensure victory and save slaughter that their profession is held in such high honour . . .

"There are many kinds of manoeuvre in war, some only of which take place upon the battlefield. There are manouevres far to the flank or rear. There are manoeuvres in time, in diplomacy, in mechanics, in psychology; all of which are removed from the battlefield, but react often decisively upon it, and the object of all is to find easier ways, other than sheer slaughter, of achieving the main purpose."

4. Clausewitz, pp. 69 and 87. It is important to recognize that military force does not replace the other elements of national power but supplements them. Clausewitz' most complete expression of his famous idea is found on page 605: "We maintain . . . that war is simply a continuation of political intercourse, with the addition of other means. We deliberately use the phrase 'with the addition of other means' because we also want to make it clear that war in itself does not suspend political intercourse or change it into something entirely different."

5. Ibid., pp. 87–88.

6. The term *annihilation* implies for many the absolute physical destruction of all the enemy's troops and equipment. This is rarely achieved and seldom necessary. Incapacitation, on the other hand, is literally what we mean to convey: the destruction of the enemy's military capacity to resist. See Hans Delbrück, *History of the Art of War Within the Framework of Political History*, trans. Walter J. Renfroe, Jr., especially vol. 4, chap. IV (Westport, CT: Greenwood Press, 1975–1985).

7. *Strategy of erosion* is known as *strategy of attrition* in classical military theory. The concepts are the same. We use the term erosion to avoid confusion with the tactical concept of attrition warfare. See Delbrück, especially vol. 4, chap. IV.

8. **Strategic level of war:** "The level of war at which a nation, often as a member of a group of nations, determines national or multinational (alliance or coalition) security objectives and guidance, and develops and uses national resources to accomplish these objectives. Activities at this level establish national and multina-

tional military objectives; sequence initiatives; define limits and assess risks for the use of military and other instruments of national power; develop global plans or theater war plans to achieve those objectives; and provide military forces and other capabilities in accordance with strategic plans." (Joint Pub 1-02)

9. **National strategy**, also referred to as grand strategy: "The art and science of developing and using the political, economic, and psychological powers of a nation, together with its armed forces, during peace and war, to secure national objectives." (Joint Pub 1-02)

10. **Military strategy:** "The art and science of employing the armed forces of a nation to secure the objectives of national policy by the application of force or the threat of force." (Joint Pub 1-02)

11. **Tactical level of war:** "The level of war at which battles and engagements are planned and executed to accomplish military objectives assigned to tactical units or task forces. Activities at this level focus on the ordered arrangement and maneuver of combat elements in relation to each other and to the enemy to achieve combat objectives." (Joint Pub 1-02)

12. **Operational level of war:** "The level of war at which campaigns and major operations are planned, conducted, and sustained to accomplish strategic objectives within theaters or areas of operations. Activities at this level link tactics and strategy by establishing operational objectives needed to accomplish the strategic objectives, sequencing events to achieve the operational objectives, initiating actions, and applying resources to bring about and sustain these events. These activities imply a broader dimension of time or space than do tactics; they ensure the logistic and administrative

support of tactical forces, and provide the means by which tactical successes are exploited to achieve strategic objectives." (Joint Pub 1-02)

13. Clausewitz, p. 357.

14. Ibid., p. 528.

15. For an excellent discussion of the attrition-maneuver spectrum and additional historical examples of attrition and maneuver, see Edward N. Luttwak, *Strategy: The Logic of War and Peace* (Cambridge, MA: Belknap Press of Harvard University Press, 1987) pp. 91–112.

16. **Combat power:** "The total means of destructive and/or disruptive force which a military unit/formation, can apply against the opponent at a given time." (Joint Pub 1-02)

17. Clausewitz, p. 194.

18. Tempo is often associated with a mental process known variously as the "decision cycle," "OODA loop," or "Boyd cycle" after John Boyd who pioneered the concept in his lecture, "The Patterns of Conflict." Boyd identified a four-step mental process: observation, orientation, decision, and action. Boyd theorized that each party to a conflict first observes the situation. On the basis of the observation, he orients; that is, he makes an estimate of the situation. On the basis of the orientation, he makes a decision. Finally, he implements the decision—he acts. Because his action has created a new situation, the process begins anew. Boyd argued that

the party who consistently completes the cycle faster gains an advantage that increases with each cycle. His enemy's reactions become increasingly slower by comparison and therefore less effective until, finally, he is overcome by events. "A Discourse on Winning and Losing: The Patterns of Conflict," unpublished lecture notes and diagrams, August 1987.

19. Clausewitz, p. 198.

20. Ibid, p. 190.

21. See Clausewitz, pp. 485 and 595–596. **Centers of gravity:** "Those characteristics, capabilities, or localities from which a military force derives its freedom of action, physical strength, or will to fight." (Joint Pub 1-02)

Preparing for War

1. Hans von Seeckt, *Thoughts of a Soldier*, trans. G. Water house (London: Ernest Benn Ltd., 1930) p. 123.

2. FMFRP 12-46, *Advanced Base Operations in Micronesia* (August, 1992) p. 41. FMFRP 12-46 is a historical reprint of Operation Plan 712 written by Maj Earl H. Ellis in 1921.

3. **Force planning:** "Planning associated with the creation and maintenance of military capabilities. It is primarily the responsibility of the Military Departments and Services and is conducted under the administrative control that runs from the Secretary of

Defense to the Military Departments and Services." (Joint Pub
-02)

4. **Doctrine:** "Fundamental principles by which the military
forces or elements thereof guide their actions in support of national
objectives. It is authoritative but requires judgment in application."
(Joint Pub 1-02)

5. Field Manual 100-5, *Tentative Field Service Regulations:
Operations*, published by the War Department (Washington, D.C.:
Government Printing Office, 1939) p. 31.

6. "In a commander a bold act may prove to be a blunder.
Nevertheless it is a laudable error, not to be regarded on the same
footing as others. Happy the army where ill-timed boldness occurs
frequently; it is a luxuriant weed, but indicates the richness of the
soil. Even foolhardiness—that is, boldness without object—is not to
be despised: basically it stems from daring, which in this case has
erupted with a passion unrestrained by thought. Only when boldness rebels against obedience, when it defiantly ignores an exress-
ed command, must it be treated as a dangerous offense; then it must
be prevented, not for its innate qualities, but because an order has
been disobeyed, and in war obedience is of cardinal importance."
Clausewitz, pp. 190–191.

The Conduct of War

1. Sun Tzu, p. 101.

2. Ibid., p. 134.

3. Sir William Slim, *Defeat into Victory* (London: Cassel and Co. Ltd, 1956) pp. 550–551.

4. **Maneuver:** "Employment of forces on the battlefield through movement in combination with fire, or fire potential, to achieve a position of advantage in respect to the enemy in order to accomplish the mission." (Joint Pub 1-02)

5. Boyd introduces the idea of implicit communication as a command tool in "A Discourse on Winning and Losing: An Organic Design for Command and Control."

6. Hence the terms *area of influence* and *area of interest.* **Area of influence:** "A geographical area wherein a commander is directly capable of influencing operations by maneuver or fire support systems normally under the commander's command or control." **Area of interest:** "That area of concern to the commander including the area of influence, areas adjacent thereto, and extending into enemy territory to the objectives of current or planned operations. This area also includes areas occupied by enemy forces who could jeopardize the accomplishment of the mission." (Joint Pub 1-02)

7. George S. Patton, Jr., *War As I Knew It* (New York: Houghton Mifflin, 1979) p. 354.

8. In the context of command and control, also called *mission command and control.* Mission tactics involves the use of *mission-type orders.* **Mission-type order:** "Order to a unit to perform a mission without specifying how it is to be accomplished." (Joint Pub 1-02)

9.   David Hillel Gelernter, *Mirror Worlds, or, The Day Software Puts the Universe in a Shoebox: How It Will Happen and What It Will Mean* (New York: Oxford University Press, 1991) pp. 51–53. If "*insight* is the illumination to be achieved by penetrating inner depths, *topsight* is what comes from a far-overhead vantage point, from a bird's eye view that reveals *the whole*—the big picture; how the parts fit together."

10.   **Mission:** "The task, together with the purpose, that clearly indicates the action to be taken and the reason therefor." (Joint Pub 1-02)

11.   Hence the terms *reconnaissance pull* and *command push*, respectively. See William S. Lind's *Maneuver Warfare Handbook* (Boulder, CO: Westview Press, 1985) pp. 18–19.

Breinigsville, PA USA
06 October 2010
246868BV00001B/10/P